WITTGENSTEIN AND REASON

Ratio Book Series

Each book in the Series is devoted to a philosophical topic of particular contemporary interest, and features invited contributors from leading authorities in the chosen field.

Volumes published so far:

WITTGENSTEIN AND REASON

Edited by
John Preston

Blackwell
Publishing

Please note chapter 1 was originally published in French as 'Wittgenstein, Critique de Frazer', Agone 23 (2000), pp. 33–54. It was translated into English (with minor editorial corrections and additional bibliographical references and abstract) especially for the present issue of *Ratio* by John Cottingham, by kind permission of Jacques Bouveresse and Editions Agone, Marseilles. English version © John Cottingham. The translator is grateful to Severin Schroeder and Christopher Wingfield for helpful corrections to an earlier draft.

First published as Volume 20, No. 4 of *Ratio*.

BLACKWELL PUBLISHING
350 Main Street, Malden, MA 02148-5020, USA
9600 Garsington Road, Oxford OX4 2DQ, UK

First published 2008 by Blackwell Publishing Ltd

1   2008

Library of Congress Cataloging-in-Publication Data

Wittgenstein and reason / edited by John Preston.
     p. cm. — (Ratio book series)
   "First published as volume 20, no. 4 of Ratio"—T.p. versp
   Includes bibliographical references and index.
     ISBN 978-1-4051-8095-5 (pbk. : alk. paper)   1. Wittgenstein, Ludwig, 1889–1951.   2. Reason.
I. Preston, John, 1957–

   B3376.W564W555455 2008
   192—dc22
   2008003439

A catalogue record for this title is available from the British Library.

Set in 11 on 12 pt New Baskerville
by SNP Best-set Typesetter Ltd., Hong Kong

For further information on
Blackwell Publishing, visit our website at
www.blackwellpublishing.com

CONTENTS

PREFACE

Versions of four of the papers featured here (those by Hanjo Glock, Jane Heal, Joachim Schulte and Crispin Wright) were presented to the one-day *Ratio* conference on 'Wittgenstein and Reason', held at the University of Reading in April 2006. The papers by Genia Schönbaumsfeld and Severin Schroeder were contributions invited for this volume. The paper by Jacques Bouveresse was specially translated for this volume by John Cottingham.

The editor would like to thank all the contributors, as well as John Cottingham and Bryan Weaver, whose editorial assistance was invaluable.

John Preston
Department of Philosophy
The University of Reading

1

WITTGENSTEIN'S CRITIQUE OF FRAZER

Jacques Bouveresse

Abstract
This paper provides a systematic exposition of what Wittgenstein took to be the fundamental error committed by James George Frazer, author of the classic anthropological work *The Golden Bough,* in his account of ritual practices. By construing those rituals in scientific or rationalistic terms, as aimed at the production of certain effects, Frazer ignores, according to Wittgenstein, their expressive and symbolic dimension. It is, moreover, an error to try to explain the powerful emotions evoked even today by traditions such as fire festivals (which may once have involved human sacrifice) by searching for their causal origins in history or prehistory; the disquieting nature of such practices needs to be understood by attending to the inner meaning they already have in our human lives. Certain important general lessons are drawn about the necessarily limited power of scientific and causal explanations when it comes to alleviating many of our fundamental perplexities not just in the area of anthropology but in philosophy as well.[1]

Drury provides the following account of the circumstances which led Wittgenstein to read and comment on Frazer's *Golden Bough*:

Wittgenstein told me he had long wanted to read Frazer's *The Golden Bough* and he asked me to get hold of a copy out of the Union library and read it out loud to him. I took out the first volume of the full edition, and we continued to read from it for some weeks. He would stop me from time to time and make comments on Frazer's remarks. He was particularly

[1] Originally published in French as 'Wittgenstein, Critique de Frazer', *Agone* 23 (2000), pp. 33–54. Translated into English (with minor editorial corrections and additional bibliographical references and abstract) specially for the present issue of *Ratio* by John Cottingham, by kind permission of Jacques Bouveresse and Editions Agone, Marseilles. English version © John Cottingham. The translator is grateful to Severin Schroeder and Christopher Wingfield for helpful corrections to an earlier draft.

emphatic that it was wrong to think, as Frazer seemed to do, that primitive rituals were in the nature of scientific errors. He pointed out that besides these (ritual) customs, primitive peoples had quite an advanced technique [skills] in agriculture, metal working, pottery etc. The ceremonies that Frazer described were expressions of deeply felt emotions, of religious awe. Frazer himself showed that he partly understood this, for on the very first page he refers to Turner's picture of the wood of Nemi and the feeling of dread that this picture arouses in us when we remember the ritual murder performed there. In reading of these practices, we are not amused by a scientific mistake but ourselves feel some trace of the dread which lay behind them.[2]

The Golden Bough does indeed begin with a description which suggested to Wittgenstein that Frazer had grasped the problem he should have tackled but in fact wholly failed to resolve:

Who does not know Turner's picture of the Golden Bough? The scene, suffused with the golden glow of imagination in which the divine mind of Turner steeped and transfigured even the fairest natural landscape, is a dream-like vision of the little woodland lake of Nemi – 'Diana's Mirror', as it was called by the ancients. No one who has seen that calm water, lapped in a green hollow of the Alban hills, can ever forget it. The two characteristic Italian villages which slumber on its banks, and the equally Italian palace whose terraced gardens descend steeply to the lake, hardly break the stillness and even the solitariness of the scene. Diana herself might still linger by this lonely shore, still haunt these woodlands wild.

In antiquity this sylvan landscape was the scene of a strange and recurring tragedy. In order to understand it aright we must try to form in our minds an accurate picture of the place where it happened; for, as we shall see later on, a subtle link subsisted between the natural beauty of the spot and the dark crimes which under the mask of religion were often perpetrated here, crimes which after the lapse of so many ages still lend a touch of

---

[2]   M. O'C. Drury, 'Conversations with Wittgenstein', in Ludwig Wittgenstein, *Personal Recollections*, ed. Rush Rhees (Oxford: Blackwell, 1981), pp. 134–5.

melancholy to those quiet woods and waters, like a chill breath of autumn on one those bright September days 'while not a leaf seems faded'.[3]

What Drury learnt from Wittgenstein on this type of question is essentially that one may mistakenly assimilate to a problem of scientific explanation what is in fact a difficulty that can be resolved entirely by the simple task of philosophical clarification:

> Frazer thinks he can make *clear* the origin of the rites and ceremonies he describes by regarding them as primitive and erroneous scientific beliefs. The words he uses are, 'We shall do well to look with leniency upon the errors as inevitable slips made in the search for truth.' Now Wittgenstein made it clear to me that on the contrary the people who practised these rites already possessed a considerable scientific achievement: agriculture, metalworking, building, etc., etc.; and the ceremonies existed alongside these sober techniques. They were not mistaken beliefs that produced the rites but the need to express something; the ceremonies were a form of language, a form of life. Thus today, if we are introduced to someone we shake hands; if we enter a church we take off our hats and speak in a low voice; at Christmas perhaps we decorate a tree. These are expressions of friendliness, reverence, and of celebration. We do not believe that shaking hands has any mysterious efficacy, or that to keep one's hat on in church is dangerous! Now this I regard as a good illustration of how I understand clarity as something to be desired as a goal, as distinct from clarity as something to serve a further elaboration. For seeing these rites as a form of language immediately puts an end to all the elaborate theorizing concerning 'primitive mentality'. The clarity here prevents a condescending misunderstanding, and puts a full-stop to a lot of idle speculation.[4]

Wittgenstein's remarks on Frazer unquestionably show a very marked preference for interpreting ritual practices in expressive and symbolic terms – a view recently defended by Beattie:

---

[3] J. G. Frazer, *The Golden Bough. A Study in Magic and Religion* [1890], abridged edition (London: Macmillan, 1922), Ch. 1, §1, p. 1. All references are to this edition, which is the one that Wittgenstein used in writing up his notes on Frazer.

[4] M. O'C. Drury, *The Danger of Words* (London: Routledge, 1973), pp. x–xi.

In my 1965 Malinowski Lecture ['Ritual and Social Change', *Man* (N.S.) 1 (1966), pp. 60–74] I developed the theme that the ideas and procedures which we generally call 'ritual' differ from those which we call 'practical' and 'scientific (or 'proto-scientific') in that they contain, or may contain, an expressive, symbolic quality, which is not found in technical thought or activity as such. I argued that even though both expressive and 'practical' modes may be and often are combined in the same course of thought or action, we need to distinguish them, for they imply different attitudes to experience, and call for different kinds of understanding. 'Practical', empirically based procedures are essentially understood when the ends sought and the techniques used by the actor are grasped. The understanding of ritual acts, however, requires in addition the comprehension of the meanings which the participant's ideas and acts have, or may have, as symbolic statements; the kinds of mental associations they involve; and the types of symbolic classification they imply. Thus, following Raymond Firth, Leach, and others, I argued that understanding religious and magical rites is in these respects more like understanding art than it is like understanding modern science. I went on to suggest that the belief in the efficacy of ritual (where, as is usually the case, it is believed to produce results) is not, like the belief in 'science' however proto-typical, based on experience and hypothesis-testing, but is rather founded in the imputation of a special power to symbolic or dramatic expression itself.[5]

Frazer's mistake is to have employed, in these contexts, a model of analysis based on means-ends rationality. He took the idea of a means employed to further a given end and applied it (or in our view more or less flagrantly misapplied it) to practices whose nature required them to be understood in a completely different way. In effect, as Nicole Belmont and Michel Izard have noted in connection with the judgement made by Frazer in *The Golden Bough* on the ceremony of the scapegoat, Frazer 'seems unaware of the whole nature and functioning of symbols.'[6] This is evidently one of the main areas where Wittgenstein thinks the judgement

---

[5]   J. H. M. Beattie, 'On Understanding Ritual', in B. R. Wilson (ed.), *Rationality* (Oxford: Blackwell, 1977), pp. 240–1.
[6]   See Frazer, *Le Rameau d'Or*, ed. Henri Peyre (Paris: Editions Robert Laffont, 1981), Vol. 1, p. xxi.

Frazer passes on the primitive and infantile outlook of 'savages' can be immediately turned back against him. Yet at the same time Wittgenstein equally reproaches Frazer for supposing that the reason why certain actions are performed in certain circumstances is always a desire to produce a certain (beneficial) effect;[7] and it is clear from this that even the explanation of ritual acts as consisting in the deployment of a symbolic power, attributed to the expressive acts in question, is in his eyes far too general. A good number of ritual actions cannot in fact plausibly be construed as resting on a belief in causal efficacy of a symbolic type, and really have no other purpose than to express something. 'Burning in effigy. Kissing the picture of one's beloved. That is *obviously not* based on the belief that it will have some specific effect on the object which the picture represents. It aims at satisfaction and achieves it. Or rather: it *aims* at nothing at all; we just behave this way and then we feel satisfied.'[8]

Wittgenstein's scepticism about our ability to construct a theory explaining ritual acts (in the broad sense) by attributing to them some goal or purpose, or some definite function, is eventually broadened to include all explanatory attempts of this kind: 'I think it might be regarded as a fundamental law of natural history that, whenever something in nature "has a function", "serves a purpose", the same thing also occurs in circumstances where it serves none, is even "dysfunctional" [*unzweckdienlich*]. If dreams sometimes protect sleep, you can count on their sometimes disturbing it; if dream hallucination sometimes serves a *plausible* end (imagined wish fulfilment), count on its doing the opposite as well. There is no "dynamic theory of dreams".'[9]

The fundamental reason why Wittgenstein condemns Frazer's explanations is not that they are false or at any rate highly contestable. It is simply that they are explanations, and that the explanation serves to prevent us seeing what should really attract our attention. In a remark from 1941, Wittgenstein says 'People who are constantly asking "why" are like tourists, who stand in front of a building reading Baedeker, & through reading about

[7] See G. E. Moore, 'Wittgenstein's Lectures, 1930–33', in Moore, *Philosophical Papers* (London: George Allen & Unwin, 1959), p. 315.

[8] Ludwig Wittgenstein, 'Remarks on Frazer's *Golden Bough*' [Part I, 1931; Part II, c. 1948; first published in *Synthèse* 1967], transl. by J. Beversluis in C .G. Luckhardt (ed.), *Wittgenstein: Personal Recollections* (Bristol: Thoemmes Press, 1996), Part I, p. 64.

[9] Ludwig Wittgenstein, from MS 137 (1948), in *Culture and Value* [*Vermischte Bemerkungen*], trans. P. Winch (Oxford: Blackwell, 2nd edn 1998), p. 82e.

the history of the building's construction etc etc are prevented from *seeing* it'.[10] This is quite close to what one might criticize Frazer for having done: his desire to find a causal explanation for what he is describing has simply made him blind to precisely those features that are, in Wittgenstein's view, the most significant ones.

In his account of the ceremony of the scapegoat, Frazer observes that 'it arises from a very obvious confusion between the . . . the material and the immaterial. Because it is possible to shift a load of wood, stones, or what not, from our own back to the back of another, the savage fancies that it is equally possible to shift the burden of his pains and sorrows to another, who will suffer them in his stead'.[11] The conception of transferring evil in this fashion is regarded as a gross error, and the practice is accordingly condemned as 'ignoble and foolish'. The spurious superiority of Frazer on this point is due to what Wittgenstein interprets as a typically modernist form of blindness to the symbolic function of the ceremony: 'People who call themselves Modernists are the most deceived of all. I will tell you what Modernism is like: in *The Brothers Karamazov* the old father says that the monks in the nearby monastery believe that the devils have hooks to pull people down to Hell. "Now," says the old father, "I can't believe in those hooks." That is the same sort of mistake the Modernists make when they misunderstand the nature of symbolism.'[12]

In his account of Wittgenstein's lectures during the years 1930–33, Moore notes that one of the principal points he wanted to underline regarding Frazer was

that it was a mistake to suppose that why, e.g. the account of the Beltane Festival 'impresses us so much' is because it has 'developed from a festival in which a real man was burnt'. He accused Frazer of thinking that this was the reason. He said that our perplexity about the reason why we are so impressed is not diminished by being informed of the *causes* giving rise to the festival, but it is diminished by the discovery of similar festivals: finding the latter can make the festival appear something 'natural', whereas this cannot happen merely as a result of being told about its causes. In this connection, Wittgenstein

---

[10]   Wittgenstein, MS 124 (1941), in *Culture and Value*, p. 46e.
[11]   Frazer, *The Golden Bough*, Ch. LV, §1, p. 539.
[12]   Drury, *Conversations with Wittgenstein*, in Rees (ed.), *Wittgenstein, Personal Recollections*, p. 122.

said that the question 'Why does this make such an impression on us?' is analogous to questions in aesthetics such as 'Why is this beautiful?' or 'Why won't this bass do?'[13]

Wittgenstein describes the explanations given by Freud as precisely 'aesthetic' in this sense, and takes issue with him for mistakenly presenting them as scientific explanations of a causal type.

The question 'What is the nature of a joke?' is like the question 'What is the nature of a lyric poem?' I wish to examine in what way Freud's theory is a hypothesis and in what way not. The hypothetical part of this theory, the subconscious, is the part which is not satisfactory. Freud thinks it part of the essential mechanism of a joke to conceal something, say, a desire to slander someone, and thereby to make it possible for the subconscious to express itself. He says that people who deny the subconscious really cannot cope with post-hypnotic suggestion, or with waking up at an unusual hour of one's own accord. When we laugh without knowing why, Freud claims that by psychoanalysis we can find out. I see a muddle here between a cause and a reason. Being clear why you laugh is not being clear about a *cause*. If it were, then agreement to the analysis given of the joke as explaining why you laugh would not be a means of detecting it. The success of the analysis is supposed to be shown by the person's agreement. There is nothing corresponding to this in physics. Of course we *can* give *causes* for our laughter but whether those are in fact the causes is not shown by the person's agreeing that they are. A cause is found experimentally. The psychoanalytic way of finding why a person laughs is analogous to an aesthetic investigation. For the correctness of an aesthetic analysis must be agreement of the person to whom the analysis is given. The difference between a reason and a cause is brought out as follows: the investigation of a reason entails as an essential part one's agreement with it, whereas the investigation of a cause is carried out experimentally.[14]

In the same way, Wittgenstein maintains that the explanation of the very special impression made on us by seeing or hearing a

[13] Moore, 'Wittgenstein's Lecture in 1930–33' in *Philosophical Papers*, p. 315.
[14] From Alice Ambrose's notes on Wittgenstein's lectures in 1932–3, in A. Ambrose (ed.), *Wittgenstein's Lectures, Cambridge 1932–35*, pp. 39–40.

description of certain rituals cannot consist in our being made aware of some hypothetical causes to be found in their history or prehistory, but depends instead on our discovering a reason we can recognize and accept as being sound, independently of any information about their real origins. Frazer thinks that the practice of fire festivals probably arises from far more ancient customs, where bonfires were used for human sacrifice:

> All over Europe the peasants have been accustomed from time immemorial to kindle bonfires on certain days of the year, and to dance round or leap over them . . . Not uncommonly effigies are burned in these fires, or a pretence is made of burning a living person in them; and there are grounds for believing that anciently human beings were actually burned on these occasions.[15]

After describing the practice of human sacrifice in the form of burning the victim on a bonfire, as is found among Celtic peoples, Frazer concludes that 'It seems reasonable to suppose that festivals of the same sort . . . were held annually, and that from these annual festivals are lineally descended some at least of the fire-festivals which, with their traces of human sacrifices, are still celebrated year by year in many parts of Europe.'[16]

As Cioffi remarks,[17] Wittgenstein has at least two distinct objections to put forward against this genetic hypothesis:

1. Frazer is wrong to believe that in order to understand what is going on we need a historical reconstruction demonstrating the existence of ancient sacrificial rights of which the present-day customs may be thought of as the distant successors. Wittgenstein maintains that, in a good number of cases, fire festivals are directly intelligible on their own. They clearly manifest their internal relation to the idea of human sacrifice, without our needing to know whether or not they trace their ancestry back to sacrifices that were really performed in times past: 'I think it is clearly the inner nature of the modern practice itself which seems sinister to us, and the familiar facts of human sacrifice only indicate the lines along which we should view the practice. When I speak of the

---

[15] Frazer, *The Golden Bough*, Ch. LXII, §1, p. 609.
[16] Frazer, *The Golden Bough*, Ch. LXIV, §2, p. 654.
[17] Frank Cioffi, 'Wittgenstein and the Fire-festivals', in Irving Block (ed.), *Perspectives on the Philosophy of Wittgenstein*, (Oxford: Blackwell, 1981), p. 213.

inner nature of the practice, I mean all circumstances under which it is carried out and which are not included in a report of such a festival. But they consist not so much in specific actions which characterize the festival as in what one might call the spirit of the festival, such things as would be included in one's description, for example of the kind of people who take part in it, their behaviour at other times, that is, their character, the kind of games which they otherwise play. And one would then see that the sinister quality lies in the character of the people themselves.'[18]

Frazer is on the way to such a solution when he remarks for example that 'in the popular customs connected with the fire festivals of Europe there are certain features which appear to point to a former practice of human sacrifice'[19] His mistake, according to Wittgenstein, is not to have asked himself enough questions about the exact nature of these features, but instead to have focused on the historical reality of the suggested connection. Wittgenstein considers that the profound and disturbing character of the practices we observe is linked for us to the fact that they directly evoke the idea of a sacrificial rite. The meaning of this has nothing hypothetical about it, and as a result it does not depend on any historical hypothesis whatsoever.

2. Frazer does not take account of the fact that the profound and gloomy nature of these ceremonies is a function of the experience they evoke in us, which allows us to impute this character to them. It all depends on the link between the behaviour we observe and our own sensations, emotions and thoughts, together with a number of things we already know about human beings and how they behave. 'Indeed, how it is that in general human sacrifice is so deep and sinister? For is it only the suffering of the victim that makes this impression on us? There are illnesses of all kind which are connected with just as much suffering, *nevertheless* they do not call forth this impression. No, the deep and the sinister do not become apparent merely by our coming to know the history of the external action, rather it is *we* who ascribe them from an experience of our own.'[20]

Or again: 'When I am furious about something, I sometimes beat the ground or a tree with my walking stick. But I certainly do not believe that the ground is to blame or that my beating can

[18] L. Wittgenstein, 'Remarks on Frazer's *Golden Bough*', Part II, p. 75–6.
[19] Frazer, *The Golden Bough*, Ch. LXIV, §2, p. 652.
[20] Wittgenstein, 'Remarks on Frazer's *Golden Bough*', Part II, p. 77.

help anything. "I am venting my anger." And all rites are of this kind. Such actions may be called Instinct-action. – And an historical explanation, say that I or my ancestors previously believed that beating the ground does help is shadow-boxing, for it is a superfluous assumption that explains *nothing*. The similarity of the action to an act of punishment is important, but nothing more than this similarity can be asserted. Once such a phenomenon is brought into connection with an instinct which I myself possess, this is precisely the explanation wished for; that is, the explanation which resolves this particular difficulty. And a further investigation about the history of my instinct moves on another track.'[21]

The fact is that when we observe a practice like the Beltane festival we do not see it as a simple innocent amusement, lacking the dimension of profundity and mystery. What the participants are trying to express is something that finds an immediate echo in certain recognisable elements in our experience, which have nothing whatever about them that is amusing or diverting. 'But why shouldn't it really be only (or certainly in part) the *thought* (*Gedanke*) which gives me the impression? For aren't ideas (*Vorstellungen*) frightening? Can't I be worried by the thought that the cake with the knobs has at one time served to select by lot the sacrificial victim? Doesn't the *thought* have something frightening about it? – Yes, but what I see in these stories is nevertheless acquired through the evidence, as well as through such things as do not appear to be directly connected with it – through the thoughts of man and his past, through all the strange things I see, and have seen and heard about in myself and others.'[22]

Instead of the idea that the rite points to some original historical sacrifice, what emerges here is simply our idea of human beings and the often strange and disturbing character of their behaviour, and everything we know already and, what is more, can readily imagine in this connection.

Wittgenstein maintains that the reply to the question raised by Frazer concerning the murder of the king-priest of Nemi – did such terrifying events occur? – is wholly contained in the question itself: 'The question "why does this happen?" is properly answered by saying: Because it is dreadful. That is, the same thing that

[21] Wittgenstein, 'Remarks on Frazer's *Golden Bough*', Part II, p. 72.
[22] Wittgenstein, 'Remarks on Frazer's *Golden Bough*', Part II, p. 79.

accounts for the fact that this incident strikes us a dreadful, magnificent, horrible, tragic, etc., as anything but trivial and insignificant, it is that which has called this incident to life.[23]

Wittgenstein asserts not only that we do not need a hypothesis concerning the origins of this kind of practice in order to understand its significance, but also that even to formulate a hypothesis of some sort is quite irrelevant in a case of this sort, where what needs to be brought into the open is the relationship in which we stand towards the practice in question, or to its surviving traces. 'Here one can only describe and say: this is what human life is like.'[24]

In saying that this is precisely what imparts the frightening aspect to the observed act that gave rise to the practice, Wittgenstein seems, as Cioffi remarks, to be proposing in his turn an explanatory hypothesis – one that is probably just as uncertain as all the others, and hence just as inadequate. 'Compared with the impression which the description makes on us, the explanation is too uncertain.'[25] That things like the murder of the King of the Forest happen just because they are terrifying is something we could easily have doubts about, if the question were put in terms of causal genesis, rather than, as is in fact the case, solely in terms of meaning. There is however at least one thing of which we can be completely sure, and which resolves any doubts we may have, namely that if we wanted to find a suitable expression for the feelings whose presence we acknowledge behind the practices we observe, then the practices themselves would provide just what we were looking for. We can of course be in doubt about whether an ancient custom does really symbolise what it appears to symbolise. But what is in no way hypothetical or uncertain is the relationship between what it appears to signify and the characteristics in virtue of which it appears to us to signify just this – what makes it appear terrifying or tragic and in no way neutral or innocent. If we wanted to find an adequate symbol to express something like the 'majesty of death', a fate like that of the king-priest of Nemi would completely fit the bill.[26] To be sure, the precise manner of expression that is chosen may largely depend on prevailing cultural conditions, and may as a result have a conventional or an esoteric

[23] Wittgenstein, 'Remarks on Frazer's *Golden Bough*', Part I, p. 23.
[24] Ibid.
[25] Ibid.
[26] Ibid.

character that is more or less marked. But Wittgenstein nevertheless maintains that, in general terms, the observed practice rests
on a connection that will end up seeming entirely natural, when
we reflect on it and perhaps also use a modicum of imagination.
Despite the horror it inspires in us, we can, even today, understand straight away the kind of thing that the practice of human
sacrifice expressed, or could have expressed.

Wittgenstein considers that our interest in ritual practices performed by peoples we call 'primitive' is connected with certain
inclinations that we feel inside ourselves, and which enable us, in
the majority of cases, to see perfectly well where they come from,
despite the impression that there is something there that requires
to be 'explained' first. It is possible that the ritual slaughter practised by the Aztecs, which plunged the European explorers into a
state of stupefaction and horror, was essentially due to an 'erroneous theory of the solar system'. But even if this explanation
given by Frazer were correct, that would still not stop us, in
Wittgenstein's view, from perceiving this practice as an appropriate way of representing and dramatizing something whose presence we feel inside ourselves. This is why what truly preoccupies us
cannot be the explanation suggested by Frazer. The reports of
human sacrifice would have an immediate interest for us, even if
the supposed facts described by those reports turned out to be
largely invented. This is because of what they reveal about certain
aspects of the human condition that we are anxious to discover,
and yet at the same time are unwilling to confront.

If our need to know in such cases does not come from a
morbid attraction towards a display of cruelty, but rather from
the desire to represent the thing clearly to ourselves in order to
make it less traumatic or less intolerable, then one could believe
that the scientific description and explanation offered by the
ethnologist might fill precisely this function, and afford us
exactly the kind of comfort we are seeking. But Wittgenstein
thinks all this is beside the point. Even if Frazer's explanation is
correct, and the ritual atrocities he describes did indeed origi-
nate in a form of ignorance that we are today completely free of,
owing to the progress of knowledge, so that there is no reason
for us to fear seeing them re-appear one day in the future, the
fact remains that the problem is less one of explaining such
strange events than of asking ourselves how we should react, and
what attitude we should adopt, in the face these alien possibilities, which attract our attention so powerfully. As Cioffi puts it,

'it is the space which the story finds already prepared for it that has to be scrutinized and understood, and not the space which the events themselves may occupy.'[27]

Wittgenstein has a strong objection against Frazer, namely that 'one could very easily invent primitive practices oneself, and it would be pure luck if they were not actually found somewhere.' To put it another way, 'the principle according to which these practices are arranged (*geordnet*) is a much more general one than in Frazer's explanation, and it is present in our own minds, so that we ourselves could easily think up all the possibilities.'[28] Hence we already in a sense possess within ourselves the principle that would allow us to devise and set up the whole gamut of primitive rites. Just as it would be an accident if we did not happen to encounter these rites somewhere in the real world, so, in a certain way, it is equally an accident that we do actually encounter some particular examples of them. What we need to understand is the quite special way in which we are affected just as much by a horrible invention or fiction as by a horrible reality, or just as much by a sinister joke as by a sinister actual occurrence. What preoccupies us is the content in itself, and not its historical reality, or the various causes that may be invoked to explain that reality.

Wittgenstein was accused by some interpreters of somehow rejecting the very idea of historical understanding, or, more exactly, of causal explanations of historical reality. But it is clear that what is in question in the 'Remarks on Frazer's *Golden Bough*' is in no way the possibility or relevance of historical explanation in general. Wittgenstein's objection is simply that such explanation cannot provide the solution to the problem we face in particular cases of this sort. It is not that we cannot immediately find some disquieting or terrifying aspect in certain seemingly anodyne practices when the idea of a particular historical origin comes to mind or is suggested to us. But in the case of the fire festivals, this aspect is not introduced by a historical hypothesis, and does not simply reside in the idea of their origins: it is a characteristic that is internal to the ceremonial action itself. The idea of burning a live human being does not belong solely to the supposed historical antecedents of the fire festivals described by Frazer, but is connected with their meaning. What makes such an impression on us

[27] Cioffi, *Wittgenstein and the Fire-festivals*, p. 233.
[28] Wittgenstein, 'Remarks on Frazer's *Golden Bough*', Part I, p. 65–6.

is not simply the idea of the possibility of the Festival of Beltane, 'but rather what is called the enormous *probability* of this thought. As that which is derived from the material'[29] – in other words, the fact that the simple presentation of the material somehow imposes the idea on our minds with irresistible force. If we find disquieting that fact that during the celebration of these fire festivals people pretend to burn a human being, this is essentially because we already know that human beings have often been burned by other human beings, and not because we are certain that, in this particular rite, real human beings were once burned. The quite special feeling we experience has no need, so to speak, to be confirmed or justified by secure historical evidence of this kind.

Wittgenstein remarks that a genetic hypothesis is often no more than a formal connection in historical guise, and it is the formal connection that is really the important thing: 'a hypothetical connecting link should in this case do nothing but direct the attention to the similarity, the relatedness, of the *facts*. As one might illustrate an internal relation of a circle to an ellipse by gradually converting an ellipse into a circle; *but not in order to assert that a certain ellipse actually, historically, had originated from a circle* (evolutionary hypothesis), but only on order to sharpen our eye for a formal connection. But I can also see the evolutionary hypothesis as nothing more, as the clothing of the formal connection.'[30]

This is why 'the correct and interesting thing to say is not this has arisen from that, but : it could have arisen this way.'[31] In numerous cases, our interest in genetic explanation is really to enlighten ourselves about the internal nature of the phenomenon itself, or to clarify the specific impression it makes on us. This is the real goal of a good number of genealogical explanations, including, for example, those of Nietzsche or Freud. They do not reveal a real relationship between two things which at first sight are unrelated, but they do suggest a formal connection between two concepts, for example between dreams and sexuality. The phenomenon that intrigues us is thus located in a context which alters its aspect more or less fundamentally. The existence of such a formal relation can correspond to a presumption that we have always had; and Wittgenstein thinks that this is what generally

[29]   op. cit., Part II, p. 79.
[30]   op. cit., Part I, pp. 69–70.
[31]   op. cit., Part II, p. 80.

happens in the case of psychoanalytic explanations, which are, according to him, almost always fairly natural, and easily give an impression of complete self-evidence. But it can equally happen that we do not accept, for one reason or another, the proposed resemblance or connection, and we challenge the explanation for its improper linking of things that do not go together at all, as for example communion and ritual cannibalism, silver and faeces, theoretical curiosity and sexual research, and so on. In such cases, our dissatisfaction will often take the inappropriate form of challenging a genetic hypothesis for its implausibility: 'Nothing proves that this is really its origin!' Wittgenstein would say that what we really don't accept is a certain formation, or transformation, of a conceptual kind.

According to Wittgenstein, an analogous effect to what we seek from genetic explanations can be obtained simply by juxtaposing certain facts with the discovery (or invention) of intermediate elements that allow us to connect things that are apparently very distant. If, for example, someone establishes a relationship between artistic creativity and sexuality, someone else may think that the idea of such a genesis is completely unacceptable, and may utterly refuse to contemplate it. Probably, in fact, only someone who is inclined for independent reasons to connect two things can be really preoccupied with the question of knowing whether there does or does not exist some genetic relationship that can be confirmed empirically. Freud persuades us to accept certain associations which we were probably not accustomed to think about before. But once our attention has been drawn to them, they can easily impose themselves on us with irresistible self-evidence, and provide us with the kind of satisfaction which we expect from a 'good' interpretation; and it is precisely this which dissuades us from trying to provide a better or alternative explanation, and which, in so doing, resolves *our* difficulty completely.

As we have seen, Wittgenstein asks himself whether the extraordinary effect produced by the detailed description of a practice like that of human sacrifice is essentially linked to the idea of cruelty towards the victim. We know, to be sure, from manifold experience, how far the behaviour of humans can be, in certain cases, bestial and inhuman: 'Nature herself imparts to humankind some instinct for inhumanity. No one makes a pastime out of watching animals play together or caress each other, whereas everyone counts it sport to watch them lacerate and dismember

each other.'[32] But the reaction we have in the present case is
manifestly not, or at least not solely, the reaction of horror and
complete incredulity that can be aroused by the spectacle of
cruelty in its pure state, exercised simply for pleasure. 'I could
hardly have persuaded myself, had I not seen it, that one could
find souls so monstrous as to want to kill people for the sole
pleasure of murdering: hacking and chopping off the limbs of
another, exercising their minds on inventing new tortures and
ways of killing, without enmity or profit, and for the sole end of
enjoying the pleasing spectacle of the piteous writhings and
groans and cries of a human being dying in agony. This is surely
the extreme point that cruelty can reach: *ut homo hominem non
iratus, non timens, tantum spectaturus, occidat* – that one human
being can kill another not out of anger, or fear, but just to watch
him dying.'[33]

We know very well that the cruelty that revolts us in the case of
certain ritual practices has virtually noting to do with the pleasure
of killing or torturing 'just to watch'. Montaigne notes that 'When
the Scythians bury their king, they strangle his favourite concu-
bine on top of his corpse, together with his cup-bearer, his groom,
his chamberlain, his bodyguard and his cook. And on the anni-
versary of his death they kill fifty horses mounted by fifty pages
who have been impaled through the spine from backside to
throat, to make a circular formation all round his tomb.'[34] The
impression made by this display of cruelty in a ceremonial context
is quite different from that which we feel in the presence of
'ordinary' cruelty. To put it another way, Frazer does not sufficiently distinguish between a ritual atrocity and any other atrocity.
His idea of a kind of cruelty that is exercised simply through
ignorance and because it is considered indispensable for attaining
a certain result, fails to take account of an essential feature of the
situation: what distinguishes ritual cruelty from ordinary cruelty is
that it stands in some figurative or expressive relation to something which in the end is much more familiar to us than we at first
suppose; this means that we have already within us an obscure
idea of the *precise reason why* these horrible acts are performed with
such solemnity.

---

[32] Michel de Montaigne, 'On Cruelty' ['De la Cruauté'], from his *Essays* [*Essais*, 1580],
Bk. II, Ch. 11; trans. J.C.
[33] Ibid.
[34] Montaigne, *Essais*, II, 12 ('Apologie de Raymond Sebond'), trans. J. C.

There is, in short, something functionally inadequate in the common talk of 'superstitions' or 'errors' in connection with primitive beliefs that are so fundamental that we cannot apply to them a description suggesting that they rest on an inadequate or non-existent foundation. 'A picture that is firmly rooted in us may indeed be compared to superstition, but it may be said too that we *always* have to reach some sort of firm ground, be it a picture, or not, so that a picture at the root of all our thinking is to be respected & not treated as a superstition.'[35] What Wittgenstein reproaches Frazer with is a total lack of comprehension or consideration for certain foundational images, whose strangeness seems to him to require an explanation at all costs. It doesn't occur to him that the 'aberrations' that he condemns and whose presence he would like to explain as far as possible could correspond to things whose sense is quite simply inaccessible to him because of his own limitations. Wittgenstein's view is that in the characteristic cases such as those studied by Frazer, the felt need for an explanation only confirms the presence of a typical form of incomprehension – incomprehension of the very kind that explanation pretends to eliminate. In a remark of 1937 he asserts that

> In religion it must be the case that corresponding to every level of devoutness there is a form of expression that has no sense at a lower level. For those still at the lower level this doctrine, which means something at the higher level, is null & void; it *can* only be understood *wrongly*, & so these words are *not* valid for such a person. Paul's doctrine of election by grace for instance is at my level irreligiousness, ugly non-sense. So it is not meant for me since I can only apply wrongly the picture offered me. If it is a holy & good picture, then it is so for a quite different level, where it must be applied in life quite differently than I could apply it.[36]

Wittgenstein one day said to Drury: 'The Cathedral of St Basil in the Kremlin is one of the most beautiful buildings I have ever seen. There is a story – I don't know whether it is true but I hope it is – that when Ivan the Terrible saw the completed

---

[35] Wittgenstein, MS 138 (1949), in *Culture and Value*, p. 95e.
[36] Wittgenstein, MS 120 (1937), in *Culture and Value*, p. 37e.

Cathedral he had the architect blinded so that he would never design anything more beautiful.'[37] Rees notes that, on another occasion, Wittgenstein explained his reaction, which is at first sight altogether astounding, by saying 'What a *wonderful* way of showing his admiration!' To which Drury had replied 'a *horrible* way.' In a case of this kind, as in that of the practice of human sacrifice, 'civilized' people like us, by concentrating in the first place on this 'horrible' or morally unacceptable (on current criteria) character of the gesture, risk completely losing sight of what it was supposed to express. As Rhees remarks, Wittgenstein could perfectly well admit that these were indeed horrible and revolting things, without this changing in any way the spontaneous reaction expressed by his comment.[38]

As Cioffi notes,[39] the most interesting question arising from Wittgenstein's remarks on Frazer is how he can accuse the author of *The Golden Bough* of having failed to resolve a problem which, in fact, he never raised. Wittgenstein underlines that someone who is troubled by the idea of ritual murder will not have his worries alleviated by an explanatory hypothesis. But Frazer does not claim to offer this kind of alleviation; he is not troubled by the idea of ritual murder, at any rate in the sense Wittgenstein thinks he should be. From Wittgenstein's point of view, there are cases where we are completely mistaken, when we believe that the trouble comes from the absence of an adequate explanation, and that the solutions depend on our acquiring supplementary empirical information that will enable us to construct a explanatory theory.

So, for example, we are mistaken when we explain the very special impression made on us by contemplating the starry sky by putting it down to the information supplied by astronomy regarding the formidable dimension of the stellar universe, the possibility that other worlds are inhabited and so on. What Pascal expresses when he says that 'the eternal silence of these infinite spaces terrifies me' could be felt well before mankind had an adequate idea of stellar distances, the vast number of worlds, and the insignificance of our own tiny world. Wittgenstein's point is that explaining the disturbing character of the fire festivals by the fact that real human beings were burnt in similar circumstances in

---

[37] Drury, *Conversations with Wittgenstein*, in Rhees (ed.), *Personal Recollections*, p. 178.
[38] Rees, *Personal Recollections*, p. 189.
[39] Cioffi, *Wittgenstein and the Fire-festivals*, p. 225

prehistoric times is the same kind of mistake as explaining the overwhelming impression made on us by the night sky by invoking ideas associated with the advanced astronomical knowledge we have acquired. 'The sinister aspect of the fire-festivals is to the prehistoric burning of a real man as the power of the starry heavens to the suggestion of astronomical facts. In both cases the enlightening, perplexity-dissipating power of a hypothesis has been misattributed.'[40]

Certainly, if someone is looking at all costs for an explanation of this kind, it is difficult or impossible to show him he is mistaken. Moreover, the fact that he is concentrating his attention exclusively on facts that are in reality irrelevant to the initial question raised can clearly postpone for a long time or even indefinitely the moment of final disillusion, when one finds oneself confronted with the phenomenon itself, in all its mystery, in the face of which one must simply agree that, as Wittgenstein put it, 'This is simply *the way human beings live*, or act, or react.'

Wittgenstein quotes a remark of Renan in his *History of the People of Israel*: 'Birth, sickness, death, madness, catalepsy, sleep, dreams, all made an infinite impression and, even nowadays, it is given only to a small number to see clearly that these phenomena have causes within our constitution.'[41] But the fact that they have their causes within our constitution does not prevent the possibility and perhaps necessity of their striking us today with just as much force. 'As though', remarks Wittgenstein, 'lightning were more commonplace or less astounding than 2000 years ago.'[42] It is true that the spirit in which science is practised today tends to remove astonishment, and indeed the very possibility of being astonished; but scientific explanations do not in themselves do this. The fact that explanation suppresses the occasions and reasons for being astonished or frightened is, according to Wittgenstein, one of the most characteristic superstitions of our scientific epoch.

The fundamental error committed by Frazer is of the same nature as the one we commit most of the time in philosophy. We mistake the exact nature of the problem we are supposed to be

[40]   Cioffi, *Wittgenstein and the Fire-festivals*, p. 219.
[41]   'La naissance, la maladie, la mort, le délire, la catalepsie, le sommeil, les rêves frappaient infiniment, et, même aujourd'hui, il n'est donné qu'à un petit nombre de voir clairement que ces phénomènes ont leurs causes dans notre organisation.' Ernest Renan, *Histoire du Peuple d'Israel* (1887–93), Vol. I, Ch. 3. Wittgenstein quotes the original French in MS 109 (1930), in *Culture and Value*, p. 7e.
[42]   Wittgenstein, *Culture and Value*, p. 7e.

resolving, and we wrongly believe that it must be resolved by the discovery of an explanation or a theory, with a risk of disillusionment that is comparable to that which besets an attempt like Frazer's – that of discovering that theories and philosophical explanations do not finally resolve philosophical perplexities in any way. Wittgenstein maintains that philosophical considerations should not in principle contain anything hypothetical; and the reason for this is that here too a hypothesis cannot furnish the mind with the kind of alleviation it seeks:

> But is it an adequate answer to the scepticism of the idealist, or the assurances of the realist, to say that 'There are physical objects' is nonsense? For them, after all, it is not nonsense. It would, however, be an answer to say: this assertion, or its opposite, is a misfiring attempt to express what can't be expressed like that. And that it does misfire can be shown; but that isn't the end of the matter. We need to realize that what presents itself to us as the first expression of a difficulty, or of its solution, may as yet not be correctly expressed at all. Just as one who has a just censure of a picture to make will often at first offer the censure where it does not belong, and *investigation* is needed in order to find the right point of attack for the critic.[43]

One could probably summarize Wittgenstein's complaints against Frazer by saying that, for him, the author of *The Golden Bough* remained stuck at a 'first expression of the difficulty' – thus giving it every chance of imposing itself on a scientific and 'enlightened' age – and that he immediately set about looking for the very kind of erroneous 'solution' indicated by his misconceived formulation of the problem.

---

[43] Wittgenstein, *On Certainty* [1949], ed. G. E. M. Anscombe and G. H. von Wright (Oxford: Blackwell, 1974) §37.

2

RELATIVISM, COMMENSURABILITY AND TRANSLATABILITY

Hans-Johann Glock

Abstract
This paper discusses conceptual relativism. The main focus is on the contrasting ideas of Wittgenstein and Davidson, with Quine, Kuhn, Feyerabend and Hacker in supporting roles. I distinguish conceptual from alethic and ontological relativism, defend a distinction between conceptual scheme and empirical content, and reject the Davidsonian argument against the possibility of alternative conceptual schemes: there can be conceptual diversity without failure of translation, and failure of translation is not necessarily incompatible with recognizing a practice as linguistic. Conceptual relativism may be untenable, but not for the hermeneutic reasons espoused by Davidson.

The later Wittgenstein is often regarded as an emblematic relativist, not least because of his influence on Winch's *The Idea of a Social Science* (1958) and Bloor's social theory of knowledge (1983), which have achieved fame in some quarters, notoriety in others. I shall disregard these trajectories here. Instead I shall link Wittgenstein's ideas to contemporary debates about incommensurability and translatability in the wake of Kuhn, Feyerabend, Quine and, especially, Davidson. I begin by distinguishing different forms of relativism, explaining why alethic and ontological relativism are both flawed and alien to the later Wittgenstein (sct. 1). Next I argue that conceptual relativism is a more plausible position, and one that was condoned by Wittgenstein (sct. 2). In section 3 I defend the feasibility of distinguishing between conceptual scheme and empirical content, provided that this is not understood mentalistically as a distinction between an organising mechanism and its raw material, but at a linguistic level as a distinction between conceptual and factual statements. Section 4 presents the Davidsonian attack on conceptual relativism. In the remainder I argue that this attack fails, partly for reasons that emerge from Wittgenstein's later work. Davidson's argument against the possibility of completely untranslatable languages fails (sct. 5). Furthermore, genuinely different conceptual schemes need not be untranslatable (sct. 6) and certain partly untranslatable practices can nonetheless be recognized as linguistic (sct. 7). The Davidsonian case ultimately rests on the idea that the preconditions of interpretation militate against the ascription of false beliefs and deviant concepts. But this 'principle of charity' is misguided (sct. 8). Whether or not conceptual relativism is ultimately tenable, it cannot be refuted purely by appeal to hermeneutic principles.

1. Varieties of Relativism

Relativism has always drawn its initial inspiration from the idea that there is significant diversity between different cultures, both diachronically and synchronically. But its claim goes beyond noting differences: there is not just diversity, we also lack neutral canons for assessing the different options as better or worse. Relativism maintains that our beliefs, concepts, or practices cannot be assessed from an impartial, universally acceptable vantage-point, since they are valid (true, justified, good, etc.) or invalid (false, unwarranted, bad, etc.) only relative to a particular individual or group of individuals (societies or even species).

Standardly, relativism is explained in cognitive terms, especially in terms of truth.[1] This *alethic* relativism holds that incompatible views all have equal cognitive value, being either all true, or none true, or each of them true for its own proponents. In this vein, Sokal and Bricmont define relativism as the claim that 'the truth or falsity of a statement is relative to an individual or a social group' (1998: 50–1; see also Siegel 1992; Boghossian 2006b). What is true for society A need not be true for society B. For example, if society A believes in witches and society B does not, then that there are witches is true for (or in) A but false for B. Thus, it has been alleged that there is no fact of the matter as to whether Native Americans originally arrived by crossing the Bering Strait, or whether they ascended from a subterranean world of spirits. Both accounts are true, the first 'for' Western

---

[1] By the same token, different forms of relativism are standardly distinguished according to the type of statement in question: factual, ethical, aesthetic, etc. (e.g. Boghossian 2006b: 13). The taxonomy here employed cuts across this established one. Alethic and conceptual relativism may apply to different types of statements or of discourse.

industrialized society, the second for certain American First Nations (see Boghossian 2006a: 1–2).

Alethic relativism suffers from several flaws. Admittedly, we occasionally speak of a belief as being 'true for' an individual or group. So we might say, for instance,

(1) That witches exist is true for society A, but that witches exist is false for society B.

But that amounts to no more than that it is *accepted* or believed by A, and it contrasts with being true *strictly speaking* or *simpliciter*. The alethic relativist, on the other hand, rejects this non-relational or 'absolutist' use of 'true'. For him *any* ascription of truth must be qualified by reference to a subject (individual or social) that accepts the belief at issue. Consequently, he is committed to the idea that the notion of truth which is in play in (1) is the same as the one that features in the following two truisms about truth and falsehood:

(2) That witches exist is true $\Leftrightarrow$ witches exist
(3) That witches exist is false $\Leftrightarrow$ witches do not exist

As a result, the alethic relativist must accept the substitution of 'witches exist' and 'witches do not exist', respectively, for 'that witches exist is true' and 'that witches exist is false' in (1). This yields

(4) Witches exist for society A, but witches do not exist for society B.

The relativist is not at liberty to gloss (4) in a harmless manner, namely as asserting that society A but not society B *believes* that witches exist. Instead, he is driven to conclude that members of A and members of B must inhabit different worlds, one populated by witches, the other not. Alethic relativism thereby lapses into *ontological* relativism, the view that even what is *real* is relative, and that different individuals or groups literally *inhabit different worlds*.[2]

---

[2] Ontological relativism must not be confused with Quine's 'ontological relativity' (1969; see Glock 2003: chs. 6–7). The latter operates at a meta-level. What is relative – in Quine's case to different 'background' theories or languages – is not (just) what is real, but the ascription of an 'ontology', i.e., roughly speaking, of *ideas* concerning what is real.

Such a radical position has occasionally been mooted by supporters of the Sapir-Whorf hypothesis in linguistics (Whorf 1956), of the incommensurability-thesis in the philosophy of science (Kuhn 1970: 134), and by Goodman (1978). But it is surely absurd. Among other things, it makes it difficult to explain how members of B-type societies could have been so successful at exploiting, oppressing and killing members of A-type societies. Are we to suppose, for example, that the bullets which colonial troops fired at the unfortunate 'natives' managed to traverse an ontological gap between different worlds before they hit their targets?

Alethic relativism is alien to Wittgenstein. In the *Tractatus* we find an obtainment theory of truth. An elementary proposition is true if and only if the possible state of affairs it depicts actually obtains (4.25; see Glock 2006). Wittgenstein later abandoned the picture theory of the proposition and with it the metaphysical apparatus of states of affairs. As a result, the obtainment theory mutated into a form of deflationism: 'For what does it mean, a sentence "is true"? "p" is true = p. (This is the answer)' (RFM 117; see also PI §136 and Glock 2004). What is common to both positions is the commitment to a form of alethic realism. By this I mean the conjunction of the following two principles:

(I)　~ (It is true that $p \Rightarrow$ it is believed/stated by someone that p)

(II)　~ (It is believed/stated by someone that $p \Rightarrow$ it is true that p).[3]

In other words, the fact that a proposition is true neither entails nor is entailed by the fact that the proposition is being stated or believed (etc.) to be true by someone, or that it would be useful to believe it, etc. Though not frightfully ambitious, alethic realism is incompatible with the idea that whether a proposition is true is relative to the beliefs of epistemic subjects.

Accordingly, Wittgenstein's account of truth never set him on a slippery slope to ontological relativism. Nevertheless, ever since Bernard Williams' 'Wittgenstein and Idealism' (1974), it has been fashionable to read into the later work a *communal* form of

---

[3]　As regards scope, we need to exclude self-referential (and arguably ill-formed) statements like 'this statement is believed/stated by someone'. (II) needs to be further restricted to exclude statements like 'Some things are stated/believed by someone'.

linguistic idealism. Nothing could be further from the truth. The suggestion that slabs, tables, stars, etc. are in any way unreal, whether as mental or linguistic entities, is anathema to the later Wittgenstein (Malcolm 1982; Glock 2007). It is wholly incompatible not just with his famous private language argument and his less well-known attack on the transcendental solipsism of the *Tractatus*, but also with the loosely speaking pragmatist and anthropological perspective he adopts. Human activity takes place within a universe which is largely not of our own making.

What is a human creation is not the world, but language and culture. So far, this is a sheer truism. It becomes problematic, though not on grounds of idealism, by Wittgenstein's insistence that no mind-independent reality dictates our concepts and practices to us, that we are free, at least up to a point, to fashion the latter according to interests and projects that differ according to historical period and cultural context.

2. Conceptual Relativism and Conceptual Schemes

This position amounts to a form of relativism, namely *conceptual* relativism. It holds that the conceptual framework we use is not simply dictated to us by reality or experience; in adopting or constructing such frameworks there are different options which cannot be assessed as more or less rational from a neutral bird's eye view.

By contrast to alethic and ontological relativism, this position admits that neither the truth-value of the statements we make nor the existence of the material world is up to us. Empirical statements are verified or falsified by the way things are, which is by and large independent of how we say they are. Their truth value is unaffected by our linguistic conventions. At the same time, what empirical statements we can meaningfully make in the first place depends on our concepts, and these in turn depend on our cognitive habits or linguistic conventions. The concepts we employ in various forms of discourse are not simply dictated to us by reality or experience. Our conceptual net does not determine whether we actually catch a fact, but it determines what kind of fact we can catch (Wiggins 2001: ch. 5). This *conceptualism* turns into conceptual *relativism* through the claim that in adopting a conceptual framework there are different options which cannot be assessed as more or less true or rational from a neutral point of view. What counts as an accurate or useful conceptual apparatus is relative to interests which may vary between individuals, disciplines and societies (e.g. Kitcher 2001: ch. 4; Dupré 1993).

In distinguishing conceptual from other kinds of relativism, I have relied on the idea of a conceptual scheme. According to Quine (1981, 41), the term 'conceptual scheme' derives from Pareto. Quine himself has used it intermittently. For example, he speaks of the 'conceptual scheme of science as a tool for predicting future experience' (1953: 42; see also 1969, 1, 24). In a similar vein, Strawson describes 'our conceptual scheme', as 'the way we think of the world', and he sets descriptive metaphysics the task of elucidating 'the actual structure of our thought about the world' (1959: 15, 9). In the wake of Quine and Strawson, numerous philosophers have employed the terms 'conceptual scheme' and 'conceptual framework' to refer to the web of fundamental notions and principles which it is the business of philosophy to investigate.

The issue of conceptual relativism is not tied to this terminology, however. There are obvious parallels between a conceptual scheme in this sense and what the later Wittgenstein calls a 'grammar'. The grammar of a language is the system of its constitutive rules, those rules which define it. Grammar includes not just rules that are grammatical in the received sense, but any rule which determines what it makes sense to say, including rules which are commonly described as syntactic, logical, or pragmatic (see PR 51; PG 60–4, 133, 143; PI §496; OC §§61–62; Glock 1996: 150–5). According to Wittgenstein, 'grammatical' rules like 'Black is darker than white' constitute our 'method' or 'form of representation'. They lay down what counts as an intelligible description of reality, establish internal relations between concepts ('black' and 'white') and license transformations of empirical propositions (from 'Coal is black and snow is white' to 'Coal is darker than snow').

Wittgenstein is a conceptual relativist. Empirical propositions are true or false depending on how things are. But the grammar of a language is *arbitrary* in the sense that it does not pay heed to any putative essence or form of reality, and that it cannot be correct or incorrect in a philosophically relevant way.

> Grammar is not accountable to any reality. It is grammatical rules that determine meaning (constitute it) and so they themselves are not answerable to any meaning and to that extent are arbitrary (PG 184).

There is room for genuinely distinct 'forms of representation', such as alternative ways of counting, calculating and measuring. Wittgenstein rejects even the modest suggestion that our form or representation is *superior* to these alternatives in any way other than a pragmatic one which is relative to certain interests. 'One symbolism is as good as the next; no one symbolism is necessary' (AWL 22; see Glock 1996: 45–50).

There are also parallels between conceptual schemes and Wittgensteinian 'grammars' on the one hand, and what Kuhn (1970) calls a 'paradigm' and Feyerabend (1975) a 'high level theory' on the other.[4] A paradigm is not a specific scientific theory, but a more general framework of concepts, problems, doctrines and methods which inform whole clusters of theories, such as classical mechanics or evolutionary biology. Under normal circumstances a single paradigm guides scientific work in a whole discipline. But during scientific revolutions incommensurable paradigms confront each other. A paradigm-shift, such as the one from classical to relativistic physics, is not simply a transition from one set of beliefs to another, but from one set of concepts and methods to another. Furthermore, such transitions do not simply lead from an objectively inferior to an objectively superior theory, but are partly dictated by extrinsic factors (social and aesthetic, etc.). By the same token, the appropriateness of a paradigm is relative to historically contingent human interests.

Kuhn's and Feyerabend's thesis that different paradigms are 'incommensurable' amounts to a radical form of conceptual relativism. It combines three claims which must be kept apart, at least initially:

conceptual diversity: there is a plurality of different conceptual frameworks, ways of making sense of experience or the world which we use either in general, or in specialized forms of discourse such as science;

epistemic incommensurability: there is no universal scientific rationality which would allow us to assess different paradigms as more or less faithful to reality. More generally, we lack a common ground for evaluating different conceptual schemes as more or less rational;

---

[4] This is no coincidence, since both were influenced by Wittgenstein. See Preston 1997 and Kindi 2006.

semantic incommensurability: different conceptual frameworks are incomparable not just as regards rationality, but also semantically. They are mutually unintelligible because one cannot translate the terms or statements of one conceptual framework into those of another.

Clearly, conceptual relativism requires not just conceptual diversity but also something like epistemic incommensurability. Furthermore, it seems that semantic incommensurability *suffices* for epistemic incommensurability. If one cannot express the claims of two conceptual schemes in a common vocabulary, it is difficult to see how one could compare them for their cognitive virtues. But as we shall see, it is far from clear that semantic incommensurability is *necessary* for epistemic incommensurability or for conceptual relativism.

3. Davidson on Conceptual Schemes

Both the arbitrariness of grammar and the incommensurability thesis involve a loosely Kantian distinction between two distinguishable elements of our experiences, our beliefs, our theories, or our discourse, namely form and content. On the one hand there is a fundamental framework or structure, a way of conceptualizing the world; on the other there are empirical data (experiences, empirical beliefs, low level scientific theories) which presuppose this framework and provide it with material to be organised. Such a contrast between scheme and content is not confined to conceptual relativists like Whorf, C.I. Lewis, Wittgenstein, Kuhn and Feyerabend. It is equally endorsed by conceptual absolutists like Strawson and, of course, Kant himself. They insist that there is a core structure of human thought to which there is no genuine alternative, at least not for creatures like us. At the same time, some contrast of this kind is prerequisite for conceptual relativism. By pain of lapsing into alethic relativism, this position must acknowledge that the truth value of empirical statements is not relative to an individual or society, whereas what statements it makes sense to make is relative to optional conceptual schemes.

It should not come as a surprise, therefore, that one can attack conceptual relativism by questioning the distinction between scheme and content. The most famous instance is Davidson's 'On the Very idea of a Conceptual Scheme' (references in parenthesis are to Davidson 1984b). He defines conceptual relativism as the doctrine that experience and/or reality are relative to a conceptual scheme and that there are, or at least could be, different conceptual schemes (183). This formulation does not distinguish diversity from relativism. Furthermore, Davidson does not keep apart conceptual relativism from alethic and ontological varieties. By the same token, he does not mention that conceptual relativism requires the scheme/content distinction on pain of collapsing into alethic relativism.

For Davidson, the connection is different. He attacks conceptual relativism by challenging the possibility even of conceptual *diversity*. There cannot be a plurality of conceptual schemes, and therefore the very idea of a conceptual scheme is vacuous. 'For if we cannot intelligibly say that schemes are different, neither can we intelligibly say that they are one' (197–8). This last step is a *non-sequitur*. To speak meaningfully of *the* conceptual scheme, as conceptual absolutism does, that scheme must be distinguishable from something else. But that something need not be an *alternative* conceptual scheme, it could also be the *content* of the one and only scheme. According to the conceptual absolutist there could not be alternatives or changes to such a scheme. But for that very reason the scheme could be distinguished from the *body of empirical beliefs*, which are constantly subject to change.

Admittedly, Davidson also challenges the dichotomy between scheme and content. He distinguishes two versions that it might take. The first, which he associates with Strawson, trades on a distinction between analytic and synthetic truths.

Using a fixed system of concepts (words with fixed meanings) we describe alternative universes. Some sentences will be true simply because of the concepts or meanings involved, others because of the way of the world. In describing possible worlds, we play with sentences of the second kind only.

Davidson repudiates this version on the grounds that the analytic-synthetic distinction is untenable. Concepts or meaning cannot be kept apart from theories about the world or content, since meaning is 'contaminated by theory'. This view has been advocated not just by Quine, but also by Feyerabend and Kuhn. To Davidson's regret, however, their attack on the version of the scheme/content distinction has encouraged them to adhere to a second version. Instead of 'a distinction within language of concept and content', they adopt 'a dualism of total scheme (or language) and uninterpreted content' (187). Accordingly, I shall speak of an internal and external version of the scheme/content distinction.

As regards the relationship between scheme and content, Davidson detects two possibilities, namely that the scheme *organizes* the content, or that it *fits* the content. For Davidson, the idea of the scheme/language fitting the world or experience ultimately boils down to the idea that its sentences are *true*, which features in the later stages of his argument. He rejects outright the attempt to explain a conceptual scheme either as 'a way of organising' experience, data, or the world, or as a 'cultural point of view'. Davidson condemns these notions as metaphorical, and so they often are, though not uniformly. In Kant, the idea that the understanding – the faculty of concepts – organises experience – the manifold of empirical intuitions – is part of an elaborate doctrine. The trouble is rather that this doctrine forms a dubious transcendental psychology, a set of quasi-empirical speculations about how the mind creates the order of nature by imposing its structure on postulated raw data (Strawson 1966; Rorty 1970).

Davidson's critique of the idea of a scheme that operates on a pre-conceptual given (whether it be the world or experience) is along the right lines, in my view. This cannot be said of his animosity towards the internal scheme/content distinction. An intra-linguistic contrast between propositions that constitute our concepts and propositions which employ concepts to make factual statements is drawn not just through the various analytic/ synthetic distinctions, but also by Wittgenstein, in terms of 'grammatical' vs. 'empirical propositions'. Along with a majority of contemporary philosophers, Davidson thinks that any such distinction is undermined by Quine's attack on analyticity. But that attack is increasingly recognized as uncompelling (e.g. Glock 2003: ch. 3). Indeed, Davidson's own argument against conceptual relativism reveals one of its flaws:

> To give up the analytic-synthetic distinction as basic to the understanding of language is to give up the idea that we can clearly distinguish between theory and language (187).

This is meant to sum up Kuhn's and Feyerabend's case against the Kantian scheme/content distinction. But Davidson himself relies on that case, and he treats the terms 'language' and 'theory' as interchangeable throughout his essay. He seems happy, therefore, to follow Quine in identifying a *language* with a *theory*, on the grounds that both are simply 'a fabric of sentences' (1960: 11; 1969: 308–11). But a language like English is *not* a theory. For one thing, the identity of a language is determined not by sentences, but by the principles for the formation of meaningful sentences, that is by syntactic and semantic rules. For another, unlike a theory, a language does not state or predict anything. Finally, even if a language were a set of sentences rather than rules for the construction of sentences, it could not be a theory. A language must contain both sentences *and* their negations, which a coherent theory cannot (Hacker 1996: 297–8; Glock 2003: 256).

If repudiating the analytic/synthetic distinction indeed leads to the equation of languages with theories, this goes to show that the analytic/synthetic distinction must be retained. The internal version of the scheme/content distinction is still in the running, therefore. It gives sense to the notion of a conceptual scheme without invoking mentalist metaphors, psychologistic doctrines or the empiricist myth of the given. Instead of postulating an organising psychic mechanism – the scheme – and a conceptually ineffable input on which it operates, it distinguishes between statements which we use to make statements of fact and statements which are of a logical, conceptual or methodological kind. The scheme/content distinction is best drawn at the level of different types of statements or of different aspects of our linguistic practices.

4. The Davidsonian Argument against Conceptual Relativism

In one respect this conclusion is congenial to Davidson, who also maintains that our best hope of explaining what conceptual schemes are is by associating them with languages. He defines a conceptual scheme as a *set of intertranslatable languages*. Consequently, a form of behaviour X would embody a different scheme from ours iff X is a language that cannot be translated into ours. Moreover, according to Davidson a conceptual scheme which *fits* the world or experience would have to be a language the sentences of which are largely true. Accordingly, a form of behaviour X embodies a different conceptual scheme – an alternative

conceptual framework that fits the world, experience or the facts–
iff X a language which is 'largely true but not translatable' (184–5,
194).

In section 8 I shall criticize Davidson's claim that we can ascribe
a language only to subjects whose beliefs we can treat as predominantly true. And as just explained, there is no such thing as a
'largely true language'. Any language must be capable of gener-
ating sentences that can be used to say things that are true and
things that are false. The real issue is whether these languages
might include some that carve up reality in ways different from
our own. Keeping this in mind, the Davidsonian argument against
conceptual relativism amounts to this:

P_1 Conceptual relativism requires the possibility of alternative
       conceptual schemes (conceptual diversity).
P_2 The possibility of alternative conceptual schemes requires
       the possibility of untranslatable languages.
P_3 We could never recognize a practice as an untranslatable
       language
C_1 We could never recognize a practice as manifesting an
       alternative conceptual scheme.
C_2 Conceptual relativism is untenable.

P_1 is obviously true. Any form of relativism presupposes that there
are diverse options of which it is possible to maintain that they are
equally legitimate. But P_2 and P_3 are false. C_1 is also false, and
while versions of C_2 may be true, this is not for the hermeneutic
reasons Davidson advances. His 'transcendental argument' for the
conclusion that natural languages are 'essentially intertranslatable' (72) misidentifies the preconditions of interpretation.

My fundamental objection can be brought out by distinguishing different and increasingly serious semantic breakdowns
between a target and a background language:

Anisomorphism: the unavailability of word-for-word translations;
Untranslatability: the impossibility of providing a translation of the
target language without modifying the background language;
Inexplicability: the background language cannot even be modified
to translate the target language, yet this is for contingent reasons;
Ineffability: the concepts or statements of the target language
cannot be translated for logical or conceptual reasons.

I shall argue that the Davidsonian argument faces a *dilemma*:

Either failure of translation means a serious breakdown like inexplicability or ineffability, then P_2 is false. *Or* failure of translation means a less serious breakdown like anisomorphism or untranslatability, then P_3 is false.

The conceptual divergences postulated by conceptual relativism can differ in scope, from local to global, depending on what parts of the respective schemes are implicated. Global divergence would separate two conceptual schemes that have *no* concepts in common. In line with P_2, Davidson conceives of local and global diversity as, respectively, *complete* and *partial* failure of translation. He denies that either alternative is genuine. A language that is completely untranslatable yet true is ruled out by Tarski's theory of truth, since the latter makes ascriptions of truth dependent on translation (194–5). Partial failure of translation is equally inconceivable, because of the preconditions of interpretation.

> Given the underlying methodology of interpretation, we could not be in a position to judge that others had concepts or beliefs radically different from our own (197).

We could never ascribe to speakers of a bona fide language a conceptual scheme that differs from our own even in parts.

Davidson does not just target such global incommensurability. To be sure, he explicitly allows that distinct *parts* of even a *single* conceptual scheme may be incommensurable. This is no coincidence, since his thesis of the anomalism of the mental commits him to the idea that the 'mental and physical schemes' are subject to 'disparate' and incompatible commitments. What he denies is that there could be two distinct *overall* conceptual schemes which diverge in even one of their respective parts (1980: 222, 243–4). So there could not be two overall schemes with divergent concepts of the mental or of the physical, respectively.

Ruling out even such partial diversity is essential to a credible attack on conceptual relativism. Few if any conceptual relativists would maintain that there could be equally legitimate conceptual schemes that differ from ours in each and every respect. And P_2 is even less plausible if it insists that any conceptual diversity implies a complete semantic mismatch. To this extent, the spectre of complete failure of translation is inessential to the Davidsonian argument. But it raises issues that are important to the more pertinent scenario of partial failure.

5. Complete Failure of Translation

Davidson's case against the idea of languages that are completely untranslatable relies on Tarski's semantic conception of truth. Tarski proposes a criterion for the material adequacy of a definition of 'true' for a particular object-language *L*, known as 'Convention T'. According to Convention T, the definition should entail for any indicative sentence of *L* a so-called 'T-sentence' of the form

(T) *s* is true iff *p*

Here '*s*' can be replaced by a name of the object-language sentence, and '*p*' by a sentence of the meta-language which translates that sentence. A definition of truth for the object-language German in the meta-language English will entail the following T-sentence, among others:

(5) 'Schnee ist weiss' is true iff snow is white.

Davidson's argument hinges on the fact that Convention T rules out definitions of truth for object-languages the sentences of which cannot be translated into the meta-language.[5]

Peter Hacker has objected that

> ... there is no essential connection between truth and translatability. Had the Tower of Babel not been built, mankind, speaking only one language, would not have been debarred from knowing and asserting truths or possessing the concept of truth (1996: 300–1).

Though correct, this observation does not refute Davidson. Even before the Tower of Babel one could have drawn a functional distinction between object- and meta-language. Even with the help of a single natural language like English Davidson can avail himself of disquotational T-sentences like

---

[5] This argument remains pertinent even when we waive the red-herring of languages that are 'largely true'. Any language, it seems, must allow for the construction of T- *and* F-sentences stating under what conditions its indicative sentences are true or false, respectively.

(6) 'Snow is white' is true iff snow is white.

Admittedly, it is a moot question whether (6) can really be said to translate from English into English. Furthermore, Hacker (299–300) is right to take issue with Davidson's claim that 'Convention T embodies our best intuition as to how the concept of truth is used' (195). Truth is a feature not of sentences (either tokens or types), but of what is said by the use of sentences. What is relative to a language is not truth, as Davidson maintains, but what is said by the use of a certain form of words. By the same token, 'true' is not a metalinguistic predicate.

To Hacker's complaints one must add that a Tarskian theory does not provide an explanation of 'true' at all. Instead, it allows one to derive T-sentences which state the *conditions* under which sentences of L are true. But this is irrelevant to the definition of truth. It is one thing to explain what the English term 'true' means. It is another thing to specify under what conditions we would call individual sentences of L true. Unlike the latter, the former does not presuppose an understanding of how the truth-conditions of the sentences of L depend on their structure and constituents. A definition of truth is responsible only to the way 'true' and its equivalents in other languages are used, not to the semantic properties of English or any other language as a whole. An explanation of truth need not tell us what the sentences of a given language mean, but only *what 'true' means.*

An analogy may help to illustrate this difference. It is one thing to know *whether* a specific legal contract is valid. It is another thing to know *under what conditions* contracts are valid in a particular legal code. And it is yet another thing to know *what it is* for a contract to be valid. The first kind of knowledge is empirical, and it corresponds to the knowledge of whether a particular sentence is true. The second kind of knowledge is a priori in the sense that it requires knowledge not of empirical facts but of a particular system of rules. It corresponds to the ability to derive T-sentences from the axioms of a Tarskian theory. But only the third kind of knowledge provides us with an analysis or explanation of what a valid contract is (what 'valid contract' means).

Consequently truth does not presuppose translation, even in the attenuated sense of disquotation. What truth *does* presuppose is truth-bearers, things that can be said or thought. This takes us right back to the original question: could there be a bona fide linguistic practice, one in which people say something true or false, but which we cannot translate into our own language?

Let us first note that the question of whether there can be languages that are *untranslatable* should be distinguished from the question of whether there can be languages that are *unrecognizable*. Rorty (1982: 5–12) characterizes Davidson's reasoning as a verificationist attack on the idea of unrecognizable languages: by excluding radically different conceptual schemes on the grounds of complete untranslatability Davidson infers that alternative schemes do not exist from the fact that we could not recognize their presence. But why shouldn't there be verification-transcendent alternative schemes? This suggestion may be supported by pointing out that even the comparatively minor change from the Ancient Greeks to us has led to a partial break-down in translatability (see sct. 7). What prevents us from extrapolating from our present situation to a 'Galactic civilization' which would count as having an unintelligible alternative conceptual scheme?

The first thing to note is that galactic civilizations *described* in our science-fiction novels *ex hypothesi* do not fit the bill. The question is whether something which transgresses the boundaries of intelligibility in such a way that we *cannot* recognize it as use of language could count as an alternative world-view. But if an anti-verificationist answers 'yes', why not suppose that contemporary bats, butterflies, trees and stars 'all have their various untranslatable languages in which they are busily expressing their beliefs and desires to one another?' (Rorty 1982: 9).

Rorty dismisses this suggestion as pointless. He has a point. Whistling in the dark, as Quine remarks somewhere, is not the proper method of philosophy. Conceptual relativism would be supremely toothless if it amounted to the claim that we cannot exclude the possibility of alternative conceptual schemes which, ex hypothesis, remain forever unrecognizable. One might also adopt a more robust, Wittgensteinian line and dismiss Rorty's scenario as downright vacuous. Our words would be meaningless without standards of application. In the case of 'language', 'believing', 'arguing' etc. these standards are provided by criteria which exclude as nonsensical application to trees. Nothing that a tree could intelligibly be conceived as doing would count as language. (Tree-beard and the ents in *Lord of the Rings* are, of course, not trees; see PI §§281–2). And this would hold equally for Galactic creatures whose nature and behaviour in no way suggest that they are speaking a language at all, translatable or not. Either response supports a version of C_2, namely that conceptual relativism is a pointless or vacuous doctrine.

Let us turn from the topic of unrecognizable languages to the topic of untranslatable languages. Contrary to Rorty, Davidson himself does not proffer the ontological claim that there cannot *be* an untranslatable language/conceptual scheme, but only the epistemological claim that we could not *have any evidence* for such a language. Against this claim, Hacker points out that there might be contingent reasons why the entire language of a community defies being translated into our own (1996: 291). Their medium of communication may be inaccessible to us. Or they might simply refuse to cooperate with our endeavours to interpret them. Still, we could recognize such behaviour as linguistic. For it would be possible to ascribe a language to a noise-making community simply on the basis of their way of life, especially if they are capable of coordinating their activities e.g. in the production of complex artefacts. Consequently the Davidsonian position on complete failure of translation is untenable, even if one rules out of court verification-transcendent languages or conceptual schemes.

6. Conceptual Diversity and Translatability

Let us turn to P_2, and hence the connection between partial conceptual diversity and partial failure of translation. Obviously, two different conceptual schemes must differ in more than mere vocabulary, i.e. in the particular sound- or inscription they use to mean something specific. German and French do not embody different conceptual schemes simply because the former uses *Hund* where the latter uses *chien*. Two languages constitute distinct conceptual schemes only if they categorize things in different ways. Furthermore, the partial conceptual diversity conceptual relativism requires involves more than incommensurability between concepts devoted to entirely different topics. The fact that the idiom of our quantum mechanics and that of our cookery books cannot be mapped onto each other does not betoken the kind of incommensurability Davidson inveighs against. An alternative conceptual scheme in his sense would have to involve *some* concepts that operate according to *different* rules – different things make sense – and yet concern the *same* region of discourse. Nevertheless, contrary to Davidson there are cases of such diversity which do not defy translation.

Anisomorphism is a familiar phenomenon from empirical linguistics, especially concerning colour vocabularies. There is no one-to-one correspondence between Russian and English colour terms, but this does not militate against compound translations such as 'light blue'. It might be held that such differences are too superficial to constitute genuine conceptual diversity. But even if this reply were in line with the letter of the Davidsonian attack, it fails for more severe cases of translatable diversity. Thus some North-American and Australian languages feature expressions for highly intricate blood-relations which can only be glossed in English through convoluted paraphrases. In other, so-called 'evidential' languages, grammar requires that any factual claim be modified by a specification of the source on which it rests. One cannot simply say, e.g., 'The book fell to the floor', since a distinction between direct observation and hearsay is an integral part of the verb phrase (Crystal 2000: 58–63). Or consider Wittgenstein's claim that divergent concepts become 'intelligible' if we imagine 'certain very general facts of nature to be different', or against the background of different forms of life (PI II. xi; RPP I §48; RFM 95). His examples include selling wood not by weight or volume but by area covered, and measuring with elastic rulers. This second case clearly involves different rules, and yet it is no less intelligible than the medieval practice of measuring by the ell.

The same goes for the pre-industrial Japanese system of measuring time, which divides into 6 spans of equal duration not a whole day but, respectively, daytime and nighttime (see Baker/ Hacker 1985: 324–5). This yields units that differ in duration between day-and night-time, in accordance with the season. For instance, a party lasting 4 units of summer day-time is longer than one lasting 4 units of summer night-time or of winter day-time. This marks an indisputable difference to our temporal units and concepts. Nevertheless, we can render temporal statements from the Japanese system in a way which is *both* accurate *and* intelligible. Instead of simply translating e.g. 'The party lasted 4 units' or 'The party lasted 8 hours' we can say 'The party lasted $4/6^{th}$ of equinox day-time'. In short, there are alternative schemes which are perfectly translatable, even without any modifications to our language.

There are also more serious semantic breakdowns, notably more severe cases of anisomorphism. Consider the following chart of colour terms in different languages (Dancy 1983: 296):

English

purple	Blue	green	yellow	Orange	red

Bassa (Liberia)

Hui	Ziza

Shona (Zimbabwe)

cips^{w}uka	citema	cicena	cips^{w}uka

Shona carves colour space up in entirely different ways. For instance, in English one cannot say that an object alters its colour in a uniform direction, yet goes from a shade of colour C_1 to a shade of colour C_1 via being a different colour C_2. But in Shona one can say that an object goes from *cips^{w}uka* to *cips^{w}uka* via *citema* and *cicena*. Rendering Shona colour vocabulary in English is a more challenging task than rendering Russian colour vocabulary. It requires elaborate paraphrase or, far better, auxiliary means such as a colour chart.

Furthermore, there are clear-cut cases of *untranslatability*, in which it is impossible to translate parts of a target language without *enriching* the background language translated into. Many of our numerical propositions and operations cannot be translated into ancient Greek, for example, without substantially modifying their numerals (Hacker 1996: 305). Indeed, it is difficult to see how the differential calculus could be glossed without the introduction of something analogous to Arabic numerals. Similarly, one would have had to introduce new concepts ('molecule', 'gene') and principles ('organisms are not regularly created from inorganic matter') into ancient Greek in order to translate recent debates in biochemistry.

The same goes for the more fraught cases familiar from scientific revolutions. Nothing prevents followers of a theory T_2 from *modifying* their conceptual apparatus in order to gloss T_1, notably by introducing new terms or constructions based on their own vocabulary. It is a moot question whether such procedures always yield synonymous phrases. But this kind of translation failure does not entail mutual *unintelligibility*, since proponents of T_2 can acquire the conceptual apparatus of T_1 without endorsing it.

Similarly in the area of metaphysics. Aristotelians and Kantians who hold to the centrality of enduring particulars are capable of mastering the 'perdurantist' idiom of space-time worms, even if they regard it as derived and confusing. 'Aetna erupted' is not synonymous to 'Part of the life-long filament of space-time taken up by Aetna is an eruption'. Nevertheless, it is obviously possible to understand both sentences and to realize that they necessarily have the same truth-value.

One might protest that such understanding need not rest on any kind of translation or explication of T_1 in T_2, however loose. Proponents of T_2 might render T_1 intelligible by immersing themselves in the old vocabulary, without being able to explicate it in their own. Alas, this leaves us with the mystifying suggestion that an individual could operate two distinct vocabularies *with* understanding, yet *without* any capacity to explain the terms of one in terms of the other to any degree. Even if such semantic schizophrenia is conceivable, it should be the last resort in accounting for the relation between different theories. Accordingly, even cases of meaning variance that constitute untranslatability are not necessarily cases of inexplicability. P_2 is wrong, because anisomorphism and untranslatability amount to conceptual diversity, yet without posing a threat to understanding.

7. Translatability and Languagehood

We must now turn to P_3, and hence to the question of whether more severe semantic breakdowns cast doubt on languagehood. Let us first consider *inexplicability*, irredeemable failure of translation for contingent reasons.

Such cases can arise for a class of expressions that Wittgenstein was the first to draw attention to, namely expressions that are defined *ostensively*, and hence by reference to *samples*. The crux is that these samples may not be available to the translators, because of a variety of factors. For instance, in the case of dead languages we may no longer know what the appropriate samples were. Thus we have difficulties translating Plato's descriptions of the Doric modes, simply because we cannot be certain about precisely what kind of instruments produced the relevant sounds. Similarly, there is a venerable puzzle about certain colour terms in some ancient Greek poetry, for instance when the sky is described as bronze or iron, or the sea as purple or wine-red. Again, in the absence of the samples we can at best speculate about the proper rendition of such sentences.[6] Even such speculation would seem rash in the fictional cases raised by Hacker (1996: 303–4). Creatures with a different colour- or sound-sensitivity, e.g. in the ultraviolet or ultra-sonic range, might employ samples we are physically incapable of employing. In that case, their colour terms would not be synonymous with any English colour terms, even if there were a way of capturing the extension of the former with the help of the latter.

What about ineffability? A first challenge is to make sense of this suggestion. As we have seen, Hacker insists that failure of translation for contingent reasons does not preclude a form of behaviour from being a language. At the same time, he concedes to Davidson that evidence for the 'logical impossibility' of translating something that appears to be speech is *ipso facto* evidence that the noises emitted are not speech at all (1996: 291). Hacker does not specify, however, what such logical impossibility is supposed to amount to.

What it cannot amount to is any contingent obstacle that arises from the external *medium* of communication. We should also exclude obstacles that arise from *cognitive* limitations. Perhaps our cognitive capacities do not suffice to acquire certain concepts from the Galactic civilization considered by Rorty. But this is no less a contingent matter than our incapacity to hear ultrasonic sounds or see ultraviolet light.

A more pertinent suggestion is that an ineffable language involves words that cannot be translated because of the way in which they imbibe their *meaning*, or simply because of the kind of meaning they have. One thing that would fit this bill is a 'private language' in Wittgenstein's sense, one which cannot be taught to others because the meanings of its signs are such that only the speaker has access to them. Such a language is *arguably* impossible for conceptual reasons, though not for the ones given in Davidson's triangulation-argument, but rather for the ones sketched in Wittgenstein's private language argument (see Glock 1996: 309–15; 2003: 289–90). At least *prima facie*, however, an ineffable language *need not* be a private one. For it *can* be shared between the members of an alien linguistic community. Neverthe-

---

[6]   Plato, *Republic* 3.33ff. Dancy (1983: 295–8) summarizes such cases, without, however, noticing their root in the use of samples.

less, it is difficult to see *why* they should be able to interpret each other while we are left in the cold, if not for contingent reasons of the kind ruled out by my definition of ineffability. What sort of meaning could be such that, because of its intrinsic nature, it is accessible to one group of speakers but not to another?

Yet another option is that untranslatability ensues not from the meaning of words but from the *messages* they are used to convey. Mystics have long since endorsed the possibility of *ineffable truths*, truths which defy expression in any language whatever. This is a position we should resist. A truth is something of which we can predicate truth, and hence something that can be expressed by a sentence and referred to by a that-clause. I do not see how something that cannot be put into words could possibly fit that bill. Even truths which have never been stated or entertained must be *capable* of being stated, at least in principle. It must be logically possible to formulate such truths in some language or other. But now, barring the contingent obstacles mentioned above, there is no reason why a truth expressible in some language should defy expression in a *suitably modified* version of English.

There may be other legitimate construals of ineffability. But on those here considered ineffability does indeed militate against languagehood. This does not salvage the Davidsonian argument, however. For it means that P_3 is defensible only if failure of translation amounts to ineffability, which renders P_2 utterly implausible.

8. Close your heart to charity

Davidson might accept the ruminations on the link between translatability and languagehood in sct. 7. But he would challenge the claims made about the possibility of translating partially distinct conceptual schemes made in sct. 4. For these run counter to his transcendental claims about the preconditions of translation. To carry conviction, therefore, a refutation of the Davidsonian argument cannot rely on initially plausible counter-examples to P_2, it must also tackle its hermeneutic presuppositions.

According to Davidson, the only way of interpreting an unknown language is to assume that its speakers hold beliefs which are by and large true. For Davidson, this 'principle of charity' is indispensable not just to 'radical interpretation', namely interpretation from scratch of an entirely unknown language, but to linguistic understanding in general.

Some proponents of charity, notably Quine, prohibit only the ascription of beliefs that are evident empirical falsehoods or explicit logical contradictions. Davidson, by contrast, occasionally favours charity 'across the board', to all types of beliefs, and entreats us to 'maximize agreement' with the interpretees. This procedure is forced upon us, he reckons, because in radical interpretation we neither know what the natives think nor what their utterances mean. Assuming that they believe what we do is the only way of solving this equation with two unknowns (1984b: xvii, 101, 136–7).

If such undiscriminating charity were legitimate, Davidson could resist the aforementioned cases of translatable conceptual diversity. The practices envisaged by Wittgenstein, for instance, would be deviant, alright, but would not constitute alternative ways of *selling* or *measuring* at all. For the differences entail that these communities do not refer to what we refer to in speaking about selling or measuring. According to Davidson, it is misguided to entertain the possibility that the beliefs of a subject about a topic X are *all and sundry* wrong; for in that case we no longer have any grounds for assuming that these views are indeed about X. 'Too much attributed error risks depriving the subject of his subject matter' (Davidson 1984a: 18).

This correct observation does not, however, support Davidson's stronger thesis that *most* of a subject's beliefs about X must be true, and that the errors we normally lumber our predecessors with are too massive:

> . . . how clear are we that the ancients . . . . believed that the earth was flat? *This* earth? Well, this earth of ours is part of the solar system, a system partly identified by the fact that it is a gaggle of large, cool, solid bodies circling around a very large, hot star. If someone believes *none* of this about the earth, is it certain that it is the earth that he is thinking about? (1984b: 168).

'Yes!' is the correct if unsolicited answer to Davidson's rhetorical question. To be speaking about the earth one does not need to be right on the scientific topics he mentions. All that is needed is an identification like: 'The vast body on which we are currently standing' or 'The body which comprises the continents and the oceans'. If someone points to the ground and says sincerely: 'We are currently standing on an enormous flat disk. If you continue walking in the same direction you'll eventually fall off the edge', he clearly believes the earth to be flat, just as we believe it to be spherical.

Davidson's undiscriminating charity is misguided. In 'domestic' communication we rightly take for granted a shared understanding of most expressions, an agreement which opens up the possibility of disagreeing in our beliefs. Even in radical interpretation the maximization of agreement is not inevitable but would lead to misinterpretation. It is wrong to ascribe opinions we take to be correct even in cases in which there is no explanation of how subjects could have acquired them. Interpretations should ascribe beliefs that it is *plausible* for people to have, whether or not they coincide with ours.

By the same token, charity poses no hermeneutic obstacle to calling the aforementioned deviant practices alternative forms of selling or measuring. The basis for this appellation is that they involve similar ways of proceeding, as in the case of selling wood by the area covered, or an analogous purpose, as in the case of different systems of measuring length or time.

Davidson has misidentified the preconditions of understanding, only slightly, but with serious consequences. Consider Wittgenstein's remark: 'If language is to be a means of communication there must be agreement not only in definitions but also . . . in judgements' (PI §242).

Davidson rightly stresses the second point, but in the process forgets the first. By insisting that we need to maximize agreement in order to understand, he puts the cart (truth) before the horse (meaning). For we must by-and-large understand what people say in order to judge whether they are speaking the truth. In the case of an alien tongue we reach such understanding not by assuming agreement in beliefs, but on the basis of shared fundamental patterns of behaviour (see Glock 2003: ch. 6.4).

9. Conclusion

The aim of this paper was *not* to vindicate conceptual relativism, but only to show that it cannot be ruled out by hermeneutic arguments against the very conceivability of conceptual diversity. It may be that the real issue is an epistemological one, namely whether there are universally acceptable standards of rationality by which to judge different conceptual schemes. For instance, the functional analogies which make it possible to describe Wittgenstein's fictional practices as alternative ways of measuring or selling may also imply that these practices are inferior ways of fulfilling these functions. In so far as the issues are semantic, however, it would seem that they concern the question of whether diverse conceptual schemes can indeed give rise to *incommensurable truth claims*. Nothing in my defence of conceptual diversity suggests that such truth-claims are possible. In so far as we can translate alternative schemes, we can also reformulate claims made in them so as to render them amenable to a test for their truth-value. And truth is not relative in the way in which meaning and concepts are.

References

Baker, G. P. and P. M. S. Hacker (1985). *Rules, Grammar and Necessity* (Oxford: Blackwell).

Bloor, D. (1983). *Wittgenstein: A Social Theory of Knowledge* (New York: Columbia University Press).

Boghossian, P. (2006a). *Fear of Knowledge: against Relativism and Constructivism* (Oxford University Press).

—— (2006b). 'What is Relativism', in P. Greenough and M.P. Lynch (eds.), *Truth and Realism* (Oxford: Clarendon), 13–37.

Crystal, D. (2000). *Language Death* (Cambridge University Press).

Dancy, R. M. (1983). 'Alien Concepts', *Synthese* 56, 283–300.

Davidson, D. (1980). *Essays on Actions and Events* (Oxford University Press).

—— (1984a). *Expressing Evaluations*, The Lindley Lecture (monograph), (University of Kansas Press).

—— (1984b). *Inquiries into Truth and Interpretation* (Oxford University Press).

Dupré, J. (1993). *The Disorder of Things* (Cambridge/Mass.: Harvard University Press).

Feyerabend, P. (1975). *Against Method* (London: Verso).

Glock, H. J. (1996). *A Wittgenstein Dictionary* (Oxford: Blackwell).

—— (2003). *Quine and Davidson on Language, Thought and Reality* (Cambridge University Press).

—— (2004). 'Wittgenstein on Truth', in W. Löffler and P. Weingartner (eds.), *Knowledge and Belief* (Vienna: öbv&hpt), 13–31.

—— (2006). 'Truth in the Tractatus', *Synthese* (148), 345–68.

—— (2007). 'Analytic Philosophy and Idealism', in J. Padilla-Gálvez (ed.), *Idealismus und sprachanalytische Philosophie* (Frankfurt: Peter Lang), 91–112.

Goodman, N. (1978). *Ways of Worldmaking* (Indianapolis: Hackett).

Hacker, P. M. S. (1996). 'On Davidson's Idea of a Conceptual Scheme', *Philosophical Quarterly* 46, 289–307.

Kindi, V. (2006). 'The Relation of History of Science to Philosophy of Science in the *Structure of Scientific Revolutions* and Kuhn's Later Philosophical Work', *Perspectives on Science* 13, 495–530.

Kitcher, P. (2001). *Science, Truth and Democracy* (Oxford University Press).

Kuhn, T. (1970). *The Structure of Scientific Revolutions* (University of Chicago Press).

Malcolm, N. (1982). 'Wittgenstein and Idealism', in G. Vesey (ed.), *Idealism: Past and Present* (Cambridge University Press), 249–67.

Preston, J. M. (1997). *Feyerabend: Philosophy, Science and Society* (Cambridge: Polity).

Quine, W. V. (1953). *From a Logical Point of View* (Cambridge/Mass.: Harvard University Press, 1980).

—— (1960). *Word and Object* (Cambridge/Mass.: MIT Press)

—— (1969). 'Replies', in D. Davidson and J. Hintikka (eds.), *Words and Objections* (Dordrecht: Reidel).

—— (1981). *Theories and Things* (Cambridge/Mass.: Harvard University Press).

Rorty, R. (1970). 'Strawson's Objectivity Argument', *Review of Metaphysics*, 207–44.

—— (1982). *Consequences of Pragmatism* (Brighton: Harvester).

Siegel, H. (1992). 'Relativism', in J. Dancy and E. Sosa (eds.), *A Companion to Epistemology* (Oxford: Blackwell), 428–30.

Sokal, A. and J. Bricmont (1998). *Intellectual Impostures* (London: Profile).

Strawson, P. F. (1959). *Individuals* (London: Methuen).

—— (1966). *The Bounds of Sense* (London: Methuen).

Whorf, B. (1956). *Language, Thought and Reality* (Cambridge, MA: MIT Press).

Wiggins, D. (2001). *Sameness and Substance Renewed* (Cambridge University Press).

Williams, B. (1974). 'Wittgenstein and Idealism', in G. Vesey (ed.), *Understanding Wittgenstein* (Ithaca: Cornell University Press), 76–95.

Winch, P. (1958). *The Idea of a Social Science and its Relation to Philosophy* (London: Routledge & Kegan Paul).

3

'BACK TO THE ROUGH GROUND!' WITTGENSTEINIAN REFLECTIONS ON RATIONALITY AND REASON

Jane Heal

Abstract
Wittgenstein does not talk much explicitly about reason as a general concept, but this paper aims to sketch some thoughts which might fit his later outlook and which are suggested by his approach to language. The need for some notions in the area of 'reason' and 'rationality' are rooted in our ability to engage in discursive and persuasive linguistic exchanges. But because such exchanges can (as Wittgenstein emphasises) be so various, we should expect the notions to come in many versions, shaped by history and culture. Awareness of this variety, and of the distinctive elements of our own Western European history, may provide some defence against the temptation of conceptions, such as that of 'perfect rationality', which operate in unhelpfully simplified and idealised terms.

We can see that what we call 'sentence' and 'language' has not the formal unity that I imagined, but is the family of structures more or less related to one another. . . . We are talking about the spatial and temporal phenomenon of language, not about some non-spatial, non-temporal phantasm. [Philosophical Investigations, §108].

1. Introduction

'Rational' (like its associates 'reason', 'rationality', 'reasoning') is a word expressing a value-laden notion, bound up with our self-image, with our views about what we are capable of and what we should aspire to. It is also a word with a long history and with many uses in many kinds of situation. So it is likely that it expresses a tangle of related concepts rather than one sharply defined notion and that more explicit awareness of the different strands and their relations could be helpful.

In the light of this there seem to be at least three potentially rewarding lines of investigation. First we can try to identify some

of the ideas and pictures currently guiding the use of the word
'rational', and to separate out some of the concepts the word is
used to express. Second we can ask what features of human life
ground the use of any concept in the 'reason/rational' group and
what we might expect of this group. Third we can try to fill in at
least some parts of the historical story in detail.[1]

In this paper I offer some thoughts on the first two questions.
On the third I shall have only speculative and sketchy remarks to
offer. I am concerned to suggest that awareness of the historical
dimension of the concepts is important and that knowledge of
actual history in our own and other cultures would be of great
interest. But I have neither the space nor the competence to
consider real history in detail.

We shall start with the first question, identifying and examining
one idea conjured up by the word 'rational', namely that of 'perfect
rationality'. Section 2 sketches the notion and some possible reactions to it. Section 3 argues that the concept has an unacceptable
presupposition, when it is thought of as something getting a grip on
us, i.e. setting a standard for actual human beings. If this is right, we
should not take the idealised notion to be the central one in the
light of which more modest notions, which do or might actually
apply to us, are defined. How then should we think of possible
more modest and applicable concepts? In search of help on these
matters Section 4 turns to our second question, speculating about
the practices which provide the context for any concepts in the
reason/rational group. Section 5 then comes back to the question
of possible understandings of 'rational' and also offers some final
speculations and suggestions.

Thoughts from the later Wittgenstein play a considerable role
in the paper. The unacceptable presupposition of 'perfect rationality' mentioned above is the truth of the picture of language in
the *Tractatus*.[2] Exploration of the more modest notions and their
possible diversity can be seen as in the spirit of later Wittgenstein-

---

[1] E. J. Craig considers the second question as applied to knowledge and shows how that
may throw light on the first in his *Knowledge and the State of Nature* (Oxford: Oxford
University Press, 1990). B. A. O. Williams approaches truth in the same spirit and also has
illuminating things to say about particular developments in the history of the notion in his
Truth and Truthfulness (Princeton: Princeton University Press, 2002). I have learnt much
from their writings.

[2] L. Wittgenstein *Tractatus Logico-Philosophicus*, first published 1921. One standard
edition in English is that translated by D. F. Pears and B. F. McGuinness (London:
Routledge, 1961).

ian ideas about the variety of language and our uses of it. It is these links which, I hope, make the paper appropriate in the context of a collection about Wittgenstein and reason. Wittgenstein himself did not talk much explicitly about reason or rationality. But he did talk about language and truth, clearly ideas which are closely related to that of reason. The kind of approach which he encourages us to adopt in thinking of language and truth might thus suggest the lines of a Wittgensteinian view of rationality and reason.

2. Perfect Rationality

Philosophers, as well as economists and others, sometimes make use of the idea of a being who is perfectly (fully, completely, ideally) rational. It is often set up in something like this way. We start by focusing on the set of a person's beliefs and desires at a given time. We then take a system of logic (e.g. classical predicate and propositional calculus) and also a decision theory. The logic and decision theory we think of as defining functions from propositional attitudes to further propositional attitudes. Thus the logic, given some set of beliefs, defines another set of beliefs, namely those the propositional objects of which are entailed by the propositional objects of the original beliefs. And similarly the decision theory, given a set of beliefs and desires, identifies an intention. Now we make a normative move. We say that a person ought rationally to believe the propositions entailed by what she already believes and ought to form the intention indicated by the decision theory as the corollary of her current beliefs and desires. With all this to hand, we are in a position to introduce the notion of perfect rationality. A person is perfectly rational, at a time and given a set of beliefs and desires, if she believes and intends (at that time, or perhaps very shortly after) all and only those things she ought to believe and intend, in the light of the original set of beliefs and desires.

What do we think about this picture of the perfectly rational person?

Some practitioners of a serious kind in logic, decision theory or the like, may want to elaborate it. For example, the sketch above traffics only in on/off belief. Perhaps we should complicate it by having our person start with degrees of belief and have her spread her confidence appropriately by Bayesian canons. Or perhaps she should reason non-monotonically as well as deductively. Perhaps we should specify that she reasons not only in accordance with the rules of propositional and predicate calculus but in accordance with the rules of some richer logic, incorporating principles for temporal, modal, epistemic or other operators. And unless our rational heroine is Robinsina Crusoe she will be seeking to co-operate or compete with other agents, whose decisions are relevant to her choices. So on the intention-forming side, it looks as if we should advance from the comparative simplicities of decision theory to the intricacies of games theory. The development of the picture is not only a matter of incorporating these complexities and working out how they might interact. It will also require adjudication between incompatible options. Will our perfectly rational person use intuitionistic or classical logic? Will she go for causal decision theory or some other version? And so on.

It is not only in these matters, of the nature of the logic and the decision/games theory concerned, that the picture invites elaboration. Other elements invite filling in, as becomes apparent when we think further about the diachronic nature of the perfectly rational being's performance. Our perfectly rational person, as we have conceived her, is like us in having some limitations. She is not omnipotent, but has to choose the best course of action from those available to her, given her limited powers. She is capable of ignorance and error about the contingent. It is only in her reasoning that she is perfect. What then is the nature of her response to any new information she gets as the result of her actions or other changes in the world? Given her fallibility, she cannot expect to learn only things which are compatible with what she already thinks and which help to fill out parts of her world view which were earlier blank or sketchy. At some points she will be faced with the need to revise her theories. But what kinds of encounters rationally necessitate revision and how should revision proceed, once it is clear that it is required? Which existing beliefs should be scrapped? What new beliefs should be added? These questions are extremely testing. Logicians, epistemologists and philosophers of science debate various possible answers to them but there is no consensus.

There is another area where some may want to elaborate the picture. What fixes the rational person's goals? We can all probably agree that reason helps us to achieve what goals we have. Hence the plausibility of including grasp of decision/games theory in our sketch of the rational person. But does rationality also help to set those goals? Perhaps, as Kantians and other ethical objectivists think, there are principles of reason (as well as or instead of the guidings of desire) which constrain and direct which of her possible projects a person can rationally endorse. If so, then the specification of perfect rationality will need to include these principles.

So one response to the sketch of the perfectly rational being is to elaborate it, drawing on the many insights and suggestions offered by the formal sciences, and by ethical thinkers, considering the various ways in which aspects of their proposals could be combined and worked through in detail.

A second (and not incompatible) reaction to the sketch is to point out that actual human beings are, for sure, not perfectly rational, however exactly that is spelled out. The first stage in specifying the perfectly rational being credited her with the power to deduce all the logical consequences of her beliefs with lightning speed. Plainly this is a power we do not have. Also rational decision making, as sketched, requires us to review all the actions we could undertake and to compare them for likely relevance to all the things we value. Again this seems an undertaking too large for our powers. Perfectly rational theory revision ratchets up the requirements yet again. It envisages the rational person as sensitive to all possible developments of her current cognitive configuration and as able to discern among them the one or ones which are rationally appropriate in the light of the new information she has just acquired. But in fact we are not even able to survey our current beliefs in such a way as to ensure their consistency. The kinds of more extensive surveys and comparisons envisaged in such theory revision are evidently wholly beyond our capacities.[3]

A third response airs a more sceptical view. Perhaps constructing the notion of perfect rationality has required us to treat various proposals as similar in shape in a way which distorts their insights. Take, for example, systems of deductive logic. The idea of entailment forms a point of entry to their study and to the related ideas of inference rule, premise, conclusion, necessity, logical truth, axiom, theorem and the like. The idea of entailment

[3]   C. Cherniak *Minimal Rationality* (Cambridge, Mass.: MIT Press, 1986); G. Harman *Reasoning, Meaning and Mind* (Oxford: Oxford University Press, 1999).

which is thus central to logic also figures in our account of what
goes on in some actual reasoning. We take ourselves to be capable
of learning one truth by seeing that it is entailed by another, so
we sometimes set out to look for entailments as a way of increasing
our knowledge. The idea of entailment thus provides a link
between logical concepts and some real human thought. It is,
however, a leap from the existence of this link to the suggestion
that deductive systems underpin the normative claims specified
earlier in the definition of perfect rationality. It is one thing to
conceive of abstract items (propositions) and to see that, considered as axioms and theorems, they exist in vast timeless patterns of
truth-value relations. It is quite another to suppose that realising
these entire timeless patterns in actual psychological configura-
tions has any claim whatsoever as a goal on the powers of a finite
creature.

If we turn to consider decision theory, it is more natural to
take it to be prescriptive. But there are also alternative ways of
seeing it. For example, it can be taken as an interpretative
framework which guides us in ascribing preferences on the basis
of actions. Or perhaps we should take it as a way of identifying
from outside the choice which presents (in some sense) the
agent's best option, but not as prescribing any particular sort of
calculation to the agent.[4]

The suspicion lurking in this third response is that the idea of
perfect rationality is a hotch potch, in constructing which we take
insights of various different shapes, derived from different philosophical enterprises, and jam them together, distorting at least
some of them as we do so. Even if one is not as hard upon the
notion as this, one may well think that it is a mere schematic shell
of an idea, with no solid life of its own. Different versions of it can
be built by putting together speculatively proposals advanced by
various lines of thought. These constructs may be useful as sim-
plifications in certain kinds of study, as for example the assumption of deductive omniscience simplifies the posing of questions
in decision theory. Or they may be playfully interesting because
they throw up more questions. But they should not be given more
serious status than this.

---

[4]   S. Blackburn considers these issues in chapter 6 of his *Ruling Passions* (Oxford:
Oxford University Press, 1998). For a helpful overview of work on practical rationality and
an introduction to the vast literature see J. Hampton 'Rationality, Practical' in E. J. Craig
(ed.) *Routledge Encyclopedia of Philosophy* (London: Routledge, 1998).

The third, sceptical, response is an estimate of the idea which may well come from those working in the various areas of philosophy from which its component elements are drawn. These practitioners are well aware of the controversial nature of their proposals and the variety of interpretations of them which may be given. Indeed they are more likely to be aware of them than those of us whose acquaintance with such work is more superficial and who may be more tempted by misapprehensions. But let us set these worries on one side, and consider another source of unease with the idea.

3. A Dubious Presupposition

Can we make sense of there being 'what perfect rationality demands of us'? If there are demands of perfect rationality then we could say that, even if we are not perfectly rational, what rationality we can in practice achieve or aspire to is defined by reference to them. So, for example, a thinker might be said to be rational (in a general dispositional sense) if she realises that there are such demands and is able to recognise and fulfil at least some of them. And the more of them a person can recognise and fulfil, the more rational she is, in a comparative sense. The fourth response now to be considered suggests that, whether or not the suspicions of the third response are justified, these ways of spelling out modest ideas of rationality will not do, because we cannot make sense of there being such a thing as what perfect rationality demands.

So let us ignore all worries of the third response, having to do with the origins of the components of the sketched idea of perfect rationality, whether they have been rightly understood and can be made to work together and so forth. Suppose that these scruples have been quieted and that we have an actual specification of perfect reasoning of the kind gestured at. Let us now ask whether it is right to say of you or me at a given time that there is some next configuration of intentional states which this perfect rationality requires of each of us.

If the standards of perfect rationality are to get a grip on us, then there needs to be a determinate starting point in us from which the demands are generated. There needs to be the thing referred to by the phrase we slipped in so easily near the start of Section 2, namely 'the set of a person's beliefs and desires at a given time'. But is there such a set? I shall now argue that there is not, since there is nothing in us which could give it secure anchorage.

If the *Tractatus* view of language and thought were defensible we could make sense of a person having the required set of beliefs and desires. The *Tractatus* picture says that there are objects, basic building blocks of all possible facts, which are labelled by simple names. And it says that, however little we are consciously aware of them, there are elements in our psychological constitution which play the role of simple names. So the question of what beliefs and desires a person has is fixed by how her simple names are configured in her psychology.

But suppose we abandon the *Tractatus* ideas of objects and simple names, what sense can we make of each of us having, at a time, a determinate set of beliefs and desires? One might propose that a person will have a repertoire of concepts (even if these are not concepts of Tractarian 'objects') and that her beliefs and desires will be fixed by the facts about how these concepts are combined.

A person's concepts, however, are not given once and for all. They are open to questioning, development and replacement. The use of any concept rests on presuppositions, for example about what it is worth aiming at or about empirical regularities in the world. As assumptions about these things change, concepts change and language develops. We may be able to achieve a point of view from which some of the presuppositions of our current concepts come into view. But each statement of such presuppositions will involve its own concepts and so its own presuppositions. There is thus no end to the project of making presuppositions explicit. The formulation of a claim which was presupposition-free would require use of concepts which are guaranteed to apply in all possible worlds, concepts which could not be inept or unusable, whatever developments occurred. It would require, in other words, the existence of Tractarian objects and our grasp of the simple names for them. But the idea of such ultimate metaphysical/conceptual simples, the referents of risk-free concepts, dissolves into incoherence when we try to think it through.

Thoughts of this kind form an important element in the reflections of the later Wittgenstein. Clearly a full exposition and defence of them is not possible here. But let us press on and see what follows if we accept them. Whatever their status, there is interest in doing this, from the point of view of imagining what the later Wittgenstein might have thought about perfect rationality, since it seems clear that he was no friend to the idea of metaphysical/conceptual simples.

Let us consider then, a person deploying in a belief a concept which has certain presuppositions. Clearly the belief itself must be included in the set on which the logic gets to work in defining the further beliefs and actions demanded of that person by perfect rationality. But should we also include in the set the presuppositions of any concept in it?

There are three options here. The first is to include the presuppositions. This then commits us to including the presuppositions of the presuppositions, and so on. And if we are right in thinking that there is no end to the unpacking of possible presuppositions this cannot yield the determinate set of beliefs and desires which we need. A second option is to include some but not all of the presuppositions. This requires a principled way of drawing the line and there seems little prospect of this. The third option is to include none of the presuppositions. We take the person's current concepts at face value, as fixed for example, by what words she explicitly deploys, and we do not delve behind this to credit her with possession of concepts only implicitly grasped or beliefs and desires which can only be articulated in terms of such implicit concepts.

But this third option too is unsatisfactory because the representation it offers of how a person takes the world to be will not capture her full complexity as a thinking being. It does not take account of those cognitive sensitivities and dispositions which are rooted in her perceptions and skills, and in her capacities for interactions with other people and with the physical environment. There is unknown potential in these things, from which new explicit concepts and ways of thinking may perhaps emerge, if circumstances are propitious. There is thus more in the intentional state of a person than can be captured by some list of linguistically expressible beliefs or desires. Such beliefs and desires are, so to speak, only the tip of the iceberg, of which the rest is the embodied and social life the person is living.[5]

---

[5]   These ideas are familiar in the context of considering the limits of artificial intelligence. H. Dreyfus has written influentially about the issue in *What Computers Still Can't Do* (Cambridge, Mass.: MIT Press, 1979) as has also J. Searle in *Intentionality: An Essay in the*

One might think that we could at least establish a core of what perfect rationality requires by applying its demands to a person's explicit beliefs and desires. But this is to overlook the potential subversive role of the as-yet-unarticulated. A person may explicitly conceptualise her situation in a way which she is capable of coming to see to be misguided. What is explicit is permeable by the inexplicit in ways which may overturn it as well as supplementing or enriching it.[6]

The conclusion of this line of reflection is that our thinking and desiring life does not go on in a form which allows the demands of deductive logic, decision theory and so on to get a direct and unproblematic grip on it. Those parts of it with which these ideas and systems fairly easily engage (e.g. linguistically expressed states) merge seamlessly into other parts where the grip becomes more and more tenuous, because those parts are not shaped in such a way as to be grist for the formal mill. There is thus is no such thing as what perfect rationality demands of me or you here and now, because there is no given, context independent, set of beliefs and desires for the demands of rationality to bite on. The phrase 'the set of a person's beliefs and desires at a time' may, indeed, be given a determinate meaning by stipulation or by some context of debate which supplies a way of interpreting it. This is often the case when such notions are employed in setting up the problems which logicians or decision theorists grapple with. But absent such stipulation or context it lacks clear reference.

4. Reasoning Animals and Their History

What other understandings of 'rational' might there be? In pursuit of an answer to this question, let us consider what features of human life make any concepts of the family of 'rational', 'reason', 'reasoning' useful to us.

When we use language, sometimes we utter one sentence alone, at some appropriate point in a stretch of action. Wittgenstein's builders, or the child buying the apples, provide

---

Philosophy of Mind (Cambridge: Cambridge University Press, 1983) and *Minds, Brains and Science* (Cambridge, MA: Harvard University Press, 1984).

[6]　Thanks to Crispin Wright and John Preston for thoughts on this issue.

examples of this.[7] But often utterances occur in the setting of other utterances, in connected discourse or in exchanges between two or more speakers. For our purposes, one particularly striking kind of exchange is this. One person produces an utterance which does not meet with acceptance, with the desired response, from its audience. Instead of agreement or compliance the speaker finds questioning or dissent. The original speaker then makes a further linguistic move, upon which, if it is found acceptable, the first move is also found acceptable. Another interesting kind of exchange occurs when people arrive at an answer to a question which interests them by exploiting what they already know and without making further empirical investigations. They articulate and pool information they already severally possess and thereby become aware of a resolution to some uncertainty. A person can also do this on her own, by articulating in proximity various different aspects of her existing grasp on the world and seeing further claims or moves which then seem proper to her.

It is in such explicit linguistic exchanges or linguistically embodied reflections, where moves are apprehended as underpinning other moves, that we find the paradigms of reasoning, of people exercising rationality. The common element in these situations is finding that some utterance is made acceptable (or unacceptable) through the making of other (acceptable) utterances. We can imagine a group of people who discuss, debate, seek to persuade each other, engage in joint investigations and the like, but do not make any explicit meta-level remarks about what they are doing. Possibly it was so with our ancestors at some point. But if people are engaging in plenty of such behaviour, they may become reflectively aware of what they are doing. They may focus on such debates and reflections, seeking to describe them and assess them, to identify their elements and their relations and to characterise those who engage in them. And it is at this point that people will find need for concepts in the area of 'reason', 'reasoning', 'rational'.

We shall return to say a little more about possible such concepts in the next section. But before that, we should note something very general about likely developments in the aspect of human behaviour we are now considering. Suppose our ances-

---

[7]   L. Wittgenstein *Philosophical Investigations* (Oxford: Basil Blackwell, 1953) §§ 1, 2.

tors engaged in linguistic exchanges and performances of the kind just indicated and became aware that they were doing so. Suppose that they began to comment on it, to note features and aspects. It is evident that things are unlikely to freeze at that point. Human beings are ingenious and inventive animals. Given time and resources (and a cultural climate not wholly set against innovation) humans will develop and elaborate their techniques and practices. We did it with ways of knapping flints, shaping fishhooks, building houses, making garments and smelting metals, where the archaeological record shows the many lines of experiment and development which have been worked through. The overwhelming probability, then, is that our linguistic practices, including the practices in the area we label 'debate', 'discussion', 'argument', 'persuasion' and the like, have undergone similar elaboration. There will have been attempts to classify, systematise, improve, elaborate, carrying on over the centuries.

These remarks are about kinds of developments which are likely to happen in a group of human beings. So they are remarks about part of the natural history of human beings, in something like a Wittgensteinian sense. But what of real history? We (i.e. analytic philosophers, in the early 21st century, in the English speaking world) have distinctively shaped ways of engaging in linguistic exchanges with each other and of thinking and feeling and behaving in connection what we do when we debate and discuss. What is the actual history of these ideas, reactions and skills?

Thinking about our own situation, we have a rich variety of ideas at our disposal about reasoning, its elements, their relations and the process of reflection. And plainly these ideas are the product of historical development. We know that our ancestors were not thinking explicitly in these terms three thousand years ago, let alone ten or forty thousand years ago. Some of the history is available to us. We study the contributions of Aristotle, Leibniz, Bernouilli, Kant, Mill, Frege, Von Neumann etc. etc. It is apparent that certain ideas crystallised and came to prominence at certain historical periods, that the products of earlier reflection fed on into later reflection and are at least one of the significant determinants of later thinking. In considering this history, we must also acknowledge that we are ignorant of a great deal. The earlier we go back the less is known. But that there has been historical change is clear. And we know also that things are still under development, because we see it month by month in the journals, where existing ideas and systems are criticised and new ones proposed. We mentioned earlier that concepts may develop, be supplemented or succeeded by others. Reflections on reasoning and attempts to generalise about it are among the drivers in that process.

Are these changes and developments homing in on the one best language and the one best way of reasoning? With technologies, for building or transport or clothing for example, there is in all probability a large space of physically feasible options, more than have been actualised by any human beings. It is contingencies, of what materials are available in the environment, what existing techniques can be easily adapted, what fits easily with other practices and values, which determine the route through this space taken by any group of people. We have no grounds for thinking it otherwise with language and reasoning.

Later Wittgensteinian thoughts, about the variety of kinds of remarks we make and the roles they have for us, provide a hospitable setting for these speculations about contingency and possible divergence. Wittgenstein invites us to become aware of the different logical shapes of concepts. Words for numbers, colours, materials, plants, sensations, actions, virtues all look much alike as words. When, however, we explore what makes the concepts these express usable for us we become aware that they are rooted in diverse aspects of the complexity of our lives and are related in contrasted ways to our interests, capacities and practices. Hence when people debate these different subject matters we would expect to find the shape and nature of possible linguistic exchanges to be equally diverse. How do such things as the syntactic structures of remarks, the previous remarks in the exchange, the presuppositions of the discussion, or the position, status and character of the speakers bear on possible relations of support? We should not expect to find uniformity in answers to these and related questions. But if there are differences in these kinds of thing, that means that people may be struck by different aspects of 'good reasoning', depending on what kinds of debates they first bring into focus. And divergences here may propagate through the later traditions. Further contrasts between groups of people, in social structures, habits of thought etc., may add to the rich possibilities for contrasted paths of development.

If the *Tractatus* picture of objects and simple names made sense we might suppose that moves to more finely differentiated vocabu-

lary and more intricately structured exchanges were moves closer
to the one ideal. We might suppose that different paths of development would converge, if pursued long enough, on the one best
language and the one best way of reasoning. But if the *Tractatus*
picture is set aside, and Wittgenstein's later outlook accepted, all
one can confidently say about various cultures' elaborations of
their concepts and tools for debating and reflecting is that they
are corollaries of changes in the lives and self-images of those
employing them. We may expect the concepts of a group to have
the shape they do at any time as a result of historical development
and to bear the marks of their history.

In opening up these historical questions we may seem to move
into non-Wittgensteinian territory. Wittgenstein is not, in general,
thought of as a historically-minded philosopher, in the sense that
he did not himself engage closely in the history of ideas. His
outlook and aims are not identical with those of others whose
work is more centrally historical, Nietzsche or Foucault for
example. But the philosophical approach of his later writing
is nevertheless open to extension in historical directions. As
remarked above, it is a fact of our natural history that we are
cultural. So part of what we remind ourselves of and acknowledge,
if we follow Wittgenstein's suggestion, are practices, pictures, feelings, ways of talking and acting, many of which we are aware of as
having a complex history. It is true that it is not possible to do
history wholly in the Wittgensteinian spirit of assembling reminders of what cannot be sensibly denied. Historical research is
bound to involve learning new things and making speculative
moves. But it can be done partly in that spirit, if one brings to it
openness to the idea that philosophical problems arise in part
because we are gripped by (mistaken) conviction that things must
be a certain way, a conviction which may be shaken by reminders
about how things actually have been and are. More knowledge of
history might help to suggest the origins, and the optional nature,
of some of the pictures which, according to Wittgenstein, hold us
captive.

5. Rationality without Perfection

We think that there is some sense in which we actually are rational. We also think that we might be more rational and, perhaps,
that we ought to be more rational. As we saw at the start of Section

3, it is attractive to unpack these modest and applicable concepts by reference to our ability to realise at least some, and to aspire to realise more, of the demands of perfect rationality. But if, as has been argued, we cannot make sense of there being such demands, then this way of unpacking any intelligible but modest notions is blocked. We need another way of explaining what sensible thoughts about ourselves we might be having when we credit ourselves with actual rationality and potential for more. If Section 4 was right about the setting of this family of concepts, help might come from considering what notions people are likely to find useful in the area of describing and appraising each other, as actual or potential participants in discursive exchanges.

There are two concepts which immediately suggest themselves. It is likely to be important to us to mark the difference between beings who can engage in reason-giving discussion and those who cannot. This is a distinction marked by one use of 'rational' – for example in the tradition which says that humans are distinguished from other animals by having reason or rationality. To enable us to think about this ability free of the associations of the word 'rational', let us find a different label for it. Let us call it 'conversability'.

A conversable being is a being with whom one can (at least sometimes) enter into dialogue, with some hope of reaching agreement or understanding. She is aware of the possibility that linguistic moves may support other moves, she is willing to offer remarks in this supportive way and is willing to respond reflectively to remarks so offered by others. She sometimes engages on her own in explicit, and at least partially verbalised, reflection about issues as a way of addressing questions which concern her. A conversable person need not, however, be naively trusting. People can make mistakes about whether or not some linguistic move provides proper support for another, and the conversable person will recognise this. So she is up for assessing reasons as well as for giving and receiving them. The conversable person thus has interests which might well lead to the development of systematic ways of representing and appraising stretches of discussion and reflection and those who engage in them.

I have argued elsewhere that there is a sense of 'rational' in which we cannot but take it that we are rational.[8] We cannot but

[8] J. Heal 'Semantic Holism: Still a Good Buy', in *Mind, Reason and Imagination* (Cambridge: Cambridge University Press, 2003).

take it that reflecting on a question, or debating about it, is likely to produce an improvement on our cognitive grasp on it. Of course we know that we are liable to make mistakes. But a person cannot take herself to be an agent unless she takes it that she has powers on which she can call and exercise of which is likely to secure the goals she has set. We have cognitive goals which we seek to secure by discussion and reflection. Insofar as we engage in discussion and reflection (and we have no conception of what it would be to live without doing so) we necessarily credit ourselves with some fair degree of competence at seeing what is relevant in reflection and responding appropriately. And possessing this competence is one thing which 'rational' could mean. This is not a distinct notion from conversability. Rather it is conversability looked at from another point of view. To see things this way is to emphasize that conversability is not just going through the motions of making claims and offering support for them without making sense to those with whom one speaks. A person is not conversable unless her remarks do, for the most part, contribute intelligibly to the enterprise of which the talking is a part.

A second likely concept arises from an interest in marking those who are particularly good at reason-giving conversing, by whatever standards their society has arrived at. This also seems to be a way we use 'rational', for example when we use it as a rough synonym for 'intelligent' 'good at thinking' or the like. But again let us invent another label for it. Let us call someone who is rational in this sense 'an impressive converser'. The impressive converser will be able to put on convincing and highly-rated performances when discussion aimed at resolving some question is going on. She is likely to be familiar with insights into good methods and appropriate standards of reflecting and discussing. She will come up with relevant supportive moves for her claims or proposals, will appreciate fully the ramifications of any new move in the discussion, will diagnose problems with the direction a discussion may be taking and draw attention to them appropriately, and so on. Her word will carry weight and her interventions will be looked to with respect.

Ability to converse impressively by the standards of their society is something most human beings could conceivably have more of. It is also, perhaps, something it would be good if most of them had more of. But a virtue of putting things in this more neutral vocabulary is that it is evidently complex and controversial whether this is indeed so. What good things are enabled by people's being impressive conversers, of the particular character which their tradition supports? What good things are threatened? If people put more of their efforts into being impressive conversers, and doing the things which are a corollary of that, would the actual upshot be one we should wish? And from what point of view? The answers to these questions are not obvious and involve both empirical and ethical reflection. The seemingly truistic nature of the claim that we could be and ought to be more rational is apt to conceal these complexities and uncertainties from us.

Each culture will have its own version of the notion of impressive conversing, if the conjectures of the last section are correct. What little we know about the origins of the European tradition of thought, and its contrasts with others, is consistent with the idea that the developments which resulted in our (21st century, analytic, English speaking) outlook represent only one possible path among many. We, in the European tradition in which Greece had a major part, seem to have been gripped very early by one sort of reasoning. This is the way of treating geometrical and arithmetical matters as topics where it is possible to demonstrate a claim, in a conclusive and context independent way, from simpler and prior claims. But other cultures seem both to have developed mathematics fruitfully in a different style and also to have located mathematics differently in their intellectual landscape.[9]

A speculation this suggests is that we, in our tradition, have approached other subject matters with our way of dealing with arithmetic and geometry as a paradigm and have looked for ways to make other subject matters amenable to calculation and proof.

---

[9]   For introductions to the history of ideas about reasoning in China and India, see the articles by C. Hansen, 'Logic in China', B. Gillon, 'Inference, Indian theories of', P. J. Ivanhoe, 'Mohist Philosophy', R. Yates, 'Mozi', all in E. J. Craig (ed.) *Routledge Encylopedia of Philosophy* (London: Routledge, 1998). For individual works which try to reconstruct detailed accounts of some aspects of early thought see R. Netz, *The Shaping of Deduction in Greek Mathematics* (Cambridge: Cambridge University Press, 1999) and K. Chemla, 'Generality above Abstraction; The General Expressed in Terms of the Paradigmatic in Mathematics in Ancient China' *Science in Context* 16, 2003, 413–458. Two collections of essays by Geoffrey Lloyd, *The Ambitions of Curiosity* (Cambridge: Cambridge University Press, 2002) and *Ancient Worlds, Modern Reflections* (Oxford: Oxford University Press, 2004) provide interesting comparisons of developments in ancient Greece and ancient China and accounts of their contrasted settings and goals. Ian Hacking also argues in his *Historical Ontology* (Cambridge, Mass.: Harvard University Press, 2002) that historical perspective in philosophy may supply valuable awareness of the contingency and variety of ways of thinking.

And as things are now, for early 21st century, English speaking, analytic philosophers, it is mastery of the distinctions and structures made available by things recognisably in this style (logic, mathematics, theory of probability, decision theory) which loom large in our view of what makes for forceful and interesting argument. When asked to define 'rational' it is to mention of these formal systems that we naturally turn. We are of course aware of the importance of qualities like inventiveness, imagination, balance, tolerance, integrity etc. in intellectual life. We may use 'rational' sometimes in a broad sense (or perhaps we use 'reasonable' instead) where we include these things in our conception of it. But our idea of being good at reflecting and discussing has its basis of operation so to speak in the formal and logical. The root of 'rational' is the Latin verb 'reri', a central meaning of which is to calculate. And the set of associations which that brings with it is still doing powerful work in our thinking. But if the earlier suggestions of Section 4 are correct, other possible and perhaps actual cultures might have their notion of an impressive converser centred differently from ours.

These speculative thoughts lead easily to others, about the origins of our notion of perfect rationality. Perhaps it is figment which we are drawn to construct, since the ingredients of it and the impulse to put them together are supplied to us by our tradition. The ingredients are the ideas about the various ways of conversing well which we have already mentioned. They include our thoughts about deductive reason, what recommends a scientific hypothesis, good ways of making decisions, how to grapple with the facts of uncertainty in judgement and so on. The impetus to put them together comes from many sources. A central one would be the grip of our mathematical paradigm, the idea that questions are best answered by finding proof of a claim, sometimes with the help of calculative procedures. But there could be other factors also, for example our theological tradition with its emphasis on perfection and unity. And perhaps other general human propensities play a role, for example for finding attractive the idea of definitive guidance which relieves uncertainty and removes responsibility. Only detailed history, of both our tradition and others, could show whether there is any truth in these speculations. What I hope to have made plausible is that later Wittgensteinian views about language and truth are congenial to ideas of this kind.

4

WORLDS OR WORDS APART? WITTGENSTEIN ON UNDERSTANDING RELIGIOUS LANGUAGE

Genia Schönbaumsfeld

Abstract
In this paper I develop an account of Wittgenstein's conception of what it is to understand religious language. I show that Wittgenstein's view undermines the idea that as regards religious faith only two options are possible – either adherence to a set of metaphysical beliefs (with certain ways of acting following from these beliefs) or passionate commitment to a 'doctrineless' form of life. I offer a defence of Wittgenstein's conception against Kai Nielsen's charges that Wittgenstein removes the 'content' from religious belief and renders the religious form of life 'incommensurable' with other domains of discourse, thus immunizing it against rational criticism.

In one of his more puzzling remarks from the *Lectures and Conversations on Aesthetics, Psychology and Religious Belief,*[1] Wittgenstein writes:

> If you ask me whether or not I believe in a Judgement Day, in the sense in which religious people have a belief in it, I wouldn't say: 'No. I don't believe there will be such a thing.' It would seem to me utterly crazy to say this. And then I give an explanation: 'I don't believe in . . .', but then the religious person never believes what I describe. I can't say. I can't contradict that person. (LC 55)

What Wittgenstein seems to be suggesting in this passage is that belief (or non-belief) in a Judgement Day cannot be characterized in terms of a difference in opinion: it is not simply a matter of negating the proposition one's interlocutor has put forward, as denying that there will be a such a thing is not, according to Wittgenstein, as unproblematic as denying that it will rain tomorrow, or, to use one of Wittgenstein's own examples, as denying

---

[1] Edited by Cyril Barrett, compiled from notes taken by Yorick Smythies, Rush Rhees and James Taylor (Oxford: Blackwell, 1966). Henceforth LC.

that there is a German aeroplane overhead (LC 53). For the religious person, Wittgenstein claims, appears to be 'on an entirely different plane' (*ibid.*). Consequently, Wittgenstein says, you can call (what the atheist believes) believing the opposite, 'but it is entirely different from what we would normally call believing the opposite. I think differently . . . I say different things to myself. I have different pictures.' (LC 55)

That is to say, if Wittgenstein is right, then atheist and believer do not diverge in opinion, but in form of life. And in this respect they are, to adapt a phrase of Davidson's, not *words*, but *worlds* apart: the believer looks at life in a different way, uses different pictures, holds other things dear than the atheist, all of which is something that goes much deeper than a simple difference in opinion does – an opinion alone does not regulate for all in one's life. This is why Wittgenstein says in a passage reminiscent of Kierkegaard: 'It strikes me that a religious belief could only be something like a passionate commitment to a system of reference. Hence, although it's *belief*, it's really a way of living, or a way of assessing life. It's passionately seizing hold of *this* interpretation.'[2]

The different ways in which such remarks have been misunderstood are notorious. They range from ascribing to Wittgenstein a kind of 'attitudinal' conception of faith whose aim is to reduce religious belief to the expression of emotional attitudes (noncognitivism) in the manner of the Logical Positivists[3] or of Braithwaite,[4] say, to the claim that Wittgenstein is advocating some kind of 'incommensurability thesis' about religious belief. Both of these views can be found, among other places, in the work of Kai Nielsen. Here, for example, is a succinct formulation of former view: '. . . the most crucial error common to both Nietzsche and Wittgenstein is to argue that Christian practice is everything and Christian belief, belief that involves doctrines, is nothing.'[5] And here is Nielsen on the latter:

The distinctive domains of discourse (e.g. science, religion, morality) *initially* give us our criteria of reasonability, justifiabil-

---

[2]   *Culture and Value*, edited by G. H. von Wright, translated by Peter Winch (Oxford: Blackwell, 1980), 64e, henceforth CV.
[3]   See A. J. Ayer, *Language, Truth and Logic* (London: Penguin, 1971), especially chapter 6.
[4]   See R. B. Braithwaite, *An Empiricist's View of the Nature of Religious Belief* (Cambridge, 1953).
[5]   Kai Nielsen, 'Wittgensteinian Fideism Revisited' in Kai Nielsen and D. Z. Phillips, *Wittgensteinian Fideism?*, (London: SCM Press, 2005), 116.

ity distinctive to each domain of discourse, but domains are not unconnected and the form of life that is there with their practices can, and should, be appealed to where some practice or practices in one domain of discourse fits or fit badly with another . . . This is what Wittgensteinian Fideism does not allow with its conception of incommensurable domains determining what constitutes a rational authority unique to each domain of discourse. Rejecting along Davidsonian lines incommensurability . . . we can assess whole domains of discourse . . . We need not, that is, be stuck with just saying that these are our practices and these are the language-games we play, this is where we stand, this is what we do around here, these are the rules we have and we can do no other.[6]

It is the aim of this paper to show that these kinds of criticism spring from a false dichotomy between 'practice' and 'belief' or between 'living a certain way' and 'believing certain things' that, if we understand Wittgenstein correctly, cannot be upheld. Consequently, *pace* Nielsen, no such thing as 'assessing whole domains of discourse' is possible, but this does not imply that religious forms of life are 'incommensurable' with other 'domains of discourse' in anything but a trivial sense. Before I press on with an explication of this, however, some more stage-setting is required and this is provided by Wittgenstein in LC right at the end of his third and last lecture. It is to this that I shall now turn.

I

A good way into the discussion that has been going on in this lecture is Wittgenstein's remark: ' "God's eye sees everything" – I want to say of this that it uses a picture . . . We associate a particular use with a picture.' (LC 71) One of the students in the lecture, Smythies, isn't satisfied with this way of putting things and objects: 'This isn't all he does – associate a use with a picture.' (*ibid.*) Wittgenstein's response to this interjection is curt since he appears to think that it betrays a misunderstanding:

Rubbish. I meant: what conclusions are you going to draw? etc. Are eyebrows going to be talked of, in connection with the Eye

---

[6]   *Ibid.*, 128–9.

of God? 'He could just as well have said so and so' – this [remark] is foreshadowed by the word 'attitude'. He couldn't just as well have said something else. If I say he used a picture, I don't want to say anything he himself wouldn't say. I want to say that he draws these conclusions (*ibid.*).

Smythies, in other words, like Nielsen, is worried that Wittgenstein's account threatens to take the 'content' – the 'doctrine' – out of religious belief. That is to say, and as Cora Diamond points out in an excellent essay, Smythies seems to think that there are only two possible ways of conceiving of the meaning of religious language: 'either we allow that people really do mean what they say in such cases (and Wittgenstein thinks that Smythies takes him to reject that alternative), or we think of them as simply expressing a resolve to live in a certain way (or something of the kind), the expression of resolve being accompanied by a picture (and Wittgenstein thinks Smythies sees him as insisting on the correctness of this alternative).'[7] Smythies' either/or is misconceived, however, for Wittgenstein isn't denying that people mean what they say when making religious utterances. Rather, he is insisting that we cannot understand what *meaning* the utterances comes down to unless we understand the *use* to which the religious 'pictures' are put. As Wittgenstein explains at CV 85e: 'Actually I should like to say that . . . the *words* you utter or what you think as you utter them are not what matters, so much as the difference they make at various points in your life. How do I know that two people mean the same when each says he believes in God? . . . *Practice* gives the words their sense.'

In passages such as these Wittgenstein is really not saying anything different than when he is, for example, tackling the philosophical (or logical) problem of what it is to mean something in the *Philosophical Investigations*[8]: 'For a *large* class of cases – though not for all – in which we employ the word "meaning" it can be defined thus: the meaning of a word is its use in the language.' (PI §43) So if Wittgenstein is denying anything in the LC, it is only the correctness of the familiar philosophical prejudice that meaning (or understanding) something consists of a peculiar 'mental

---

[7] 'Wittgenstein on Religious Belief: The Gulfs Between Us' in *Religion and Wittgenstein's Legacy* edited by D. Z. Phillips and Mario von der Ruhr (Aldershot: Ashgate 2005), 118.

[8] Edited by G. E. M. Anscombe, Rush Rhees and G. H. von Wright (Oxford: Blackwell, 1958), translated by G. E. M. Anscombe; henceforth PI.

process': 'In our failure to understand the use of a word we take it as the expression of a queer *process.*' (PI §196) This explains why, in lecture III of LC, we get the apparent *non sequitur* of Wittgenstein suddenly asking, after a brief discussion of what it would be like to imagine oneself as a disembodied spirit, 'If you think of your brother in America, how do you know that what you think is, that the thought inside you is, of your brother being in America? Is this an experiential business?' (LC 66)

Wittgenstein is compelled to ask these questions at this point in the discussion, as Smythies has fallen into the trap of believing that you can talk of understanding a word 'without any reference to the technique of its usage' (LC 68). And the significance of Wittgenstein's interpolation is precisely to show that just as you cannot, as it were, 'read off' from your thought that it is the thought of your brother in America, so you can't find out the meaning of words (or sentences) by inspecting what goes on inside you while you utter (or 'mean') them. For, as Wittgenstein asks, 'What is the connection between these words, or anything, substitutable for them, with my brother in America?' (LC 67)

Smythies seems to think that when it comes to thought, we can be absolutely sure, right from the start (and independently of any sense-giving context), that *this* is a thought of *that* – as if 'thought' were an international, self-interpreting sign-language which left no question of interpretation (or connection) open, or as if it were a kind of 'super-picture' (LC 67) of reality that required no 'method of projection' in order to be understood. But, as Wittgenstein points out in the *Lectures on Aesthetics*, 'If a Frenchman says: "It is raining" in French and an Englishman also says it in English, it is not that something happens in both minds which is the real sense of "It is raining".' Rather, '(1) Thinking (or imagery) is not an accompaniment of the words as they are spoken or heard; (2) The sense – the thought "It's raining" – is not even the words *with* the accompaniment of some sort of imagery. It *is* the thought "It's raining" only within the English language.' (LC 30) That is to say, by ruling out options (1) and (2), Wittgenstein is also rejecting both sides of Smythies' dichotomy: meaning a word or phrase is not a mental 'accompaniment' to the written or spoken words and neither does it consist of merely acting in a certain way '*with* the accompaniment of some sort of imagery' – the conception Smythies erroneously believes Wittgenstein has in mind when he says that the person who says 'God's eye sees everything' is associating a particular use with a picture. This is why, in the *Brown Book*, Wittgenstein calls it 'a kind of general disease of thinking' to believe that meaning something is 'a mental state from which all our acts spring as from a reservoir'.[9]

Consequently, Wittgenstein is not denying that the religious person means what he says (as Smythies believes), but is rather rejecting Smythies' conception of what meaning something consists in. In other words, far from holding that the religious person *only* uses a picture – as opposed to something better – Wittgenstein insists that 'the whole *weight* may be in the picture.' (LC 72) But what does this mean? In the PI Wittgenstein gives us some helpful clues:

> If we compare a proposition to a picture, we must think whether we are comparing it to a portrait (a historical representation) or to a genre-picture. And both comparisons have point. When I look at a genre-picture, it 'tells' me something, even though I don't believe (imagine) for a moment that the people I see in it really exist, or that there have really been people in that situation. But suppose I ask: '*What* does it tell me then?' I should like to say 'What the picture tells me is itself.' That is, its telling me something consists in its own structure, in *its* own lines and colours. (PI §522–23)

In other words, Wittgenstein is suggesting here that there are two ways that a picture, and consequently, if his analogy is correct, a sentence, can 'tell' me something. It can either tell me something in the way that a historical portrait depicts a historical event – something that can also be described without using the picture – or it can 'tell' me something in a way that is not specifiable independently of the picture itself. Wittgenstein explains:

> We speak of understanding a sentence in the sense in which it can be replaced by another which says the same; but also in the sense in which it cannot be replaced by any other. (Any more than one musical theme can be replaced by another.) In the one case the thought in the sentence is something common to different sentences; in the other, something that is expressed only by these words in these positions. (Understanding a poem.) (PI §531)

---

[9]   Ludwig Wittgenstein, *The Blue and Brown Books* (New York: Harper and Row, 1965), 143.

Now when Wittgenstein says to Smythies that the whole weight may be in the picture, I believe that what he means is that the sentence in question cannot straightforwardly be replaced by another 'which says the same' and hence that the picture is irreplaceable in the sense of being non-paraphrasable. This is why Wittgenstein says:

> Isn't it as important as anything else, what picture he does use? Of certain pictures we say that they might just as well be replaced by another – e.g. we could, under certain circumstances, have one projection of an ellipse drawn instead of another. [He *may* say]: 'I would have been prepared to use another picture, it would have had the same effect'. . . (LC 71)

In this example the picture employed is therefore *not* essential to what is being communicated – it is not irreplaceable – for it can easily be swapped for another which 'has the same effect'. In this respect, to borrow Aaron Ridley's terminology, the picture is 'instrumentally intersubstitutable'[10] – it can be replaced by another which says the same thing (or brings about the same end). I take it that it is Smythies' worry that this is how Wittgenstein conceives of *all* pictures, namely, as being merely the means to some independently specifiable end (such as, say, living in a certain way[11]), whereas the whole point of Wittgenstein's distinction between 'essential' (irreplaceable/non-paraphrasable) and 'inessential' (replaceable/paraphrasable) pictures in LC is precisely to show that 'religious pictures' are *not* instrumentally intersubstitutable in the way that Smythies fears.

Naturally, when Wittgenstein says in the aforementioned passage from the PI that in the case of 'paraphrasable' sentences 'the thought in the sentence is something common to different sentences', while in the non-substitutable case 'the thought' can be 'expressed only by these words in these positions', we must not take this to mean, *à la* Smythies, that 'the thought' is something over and above *all* the sentences in which it occurs. That is to say, there is no way of 'independently specifying the thought' short of offering another sentence that also conveys it. As Wittgenstein says

---

[10] See *The Philosophy of Music. Theme and Variations* (Edinburgh: Edinburgh University Press, 2004), 28.
[11] Compare also Diamond's list of examples of the nonessential use of pictures in her 'Wittgenstein on Religious Belief', 119.

in 1931 in CV – still using the vestiges of Tractarian terminology –
'The limit of language is shown by its being impossible to describe
the fact which corresponds to (is the translation of) a sentence,
without simply repeating the sentence.'(CV 10e) Of course, as
Wittgenstein later realized, there is nothing mysterious or
'limiting' about this fact about thought at all. For the idea that
'thoughts' (or 'facts') should be specifiable independently of language use is only lent credence by the incoherent 'mental process'
picture of thought. If, however, as Wittgenstein says, we come to
recognize that the thought 'it is raining' only is *this thought* within
the English language (LC 30), then it becomes perfectly obvious
why there is no other way of saying 'it is raining' than by saying
'it is raining' or employing some paraphrase thereof – such as,
for instance, to adapt a French expression, 'it is pissing from
the sky'.[12]

That is to say, the point of Wittgenstein's distinction between
the essential and the inessential use of pictures (sentences) is not
to draw a distinction between sentences which can and sentences
which can't latch onto independently specifiable thoughts or
facts. Neither, therefore, is it to make a distinction between language use which 'refers' to reality and language use which
doesn't. In other words, and *contra* most – including Smythies' –
misreadings of him, Wittgenstein is *not*, as Putnam emphasizes,
saying the following: 'in ordinary language we have pictures (and,
of course, words) and uses of pictures and words, *and* something
beyond the words and pictures, while in religious language we
have only pictures and words and uses of pictures and words.'[13]
We only ever have pictures and words and uses of pictures and
words. There is no such thing as 'latching onto reality' *simpliciter*,
say by correlating words with 'transcendent' or 'mental' objects
that are supposed to 'anchor' our language to a non-linguistic
'beyond' (*pace* the author of TLP).[14] In this respect religious

---

[12] The expression is 'il pleut à vache qui pisse' which of course wouldn't be a paraphrase, but a qualification.

[13] See Hilary Putnam, *Renewing Philosophy* (Harvard: Harvard University Press, 1992),
159.

[14] I.e. what Wittgenstein is rejecting here is the view that in ordinary language the
meaning of a word is the object it stands for, while in religious language there is nothing
for which the words stand and they therefore refer, at best, to emotional attitudes. That is
to say, Wittgenstein is both rejecting a naïve realism as well as a naïve anti-realism about
language here, he is not saying something Derrida-esque such as 'there is nothing outside
the text'.

language is no different from non-religious language. Where it *is* different, according to Wittgenstein, is that in the religious case I cannot do without the picture, I cannot describe my use of the picture without using the picture,[15] whereas in 'ordinary' language, I often can do without the 'picture' (or without this particular turn of phrase – but not, of course, as we have just seen, without *any* form of words) and use something else, a different picture or another form of words, instead. In this sense 'ordinary' language is often 'instrumentally intersubstitutable', whereas religious language (generally) isn't. And this is a feature that religious language shares with aesthetic language use – hence Wittgenstein's aside at PI §531 about 'understanding a poem'.

Two different senses of the word 'understanding' can therefore be distinguished which mirror the 'essential' and 'inessential' use of pictures just described. Following Ridley, I will call these two different senses 'internal' and 'external' understanding respectively. That is to say, Wittgenstein's notion of understanding a sentence 'in the sense in which it cannot be replaced by any other' (PI §531) will be called 'internal', to register the fact, as Ridley says, 'that what is grasped in it is, because "expressed only by these words in these positions", understood as internal to *this* particular arrangement of words',[16] whereas understanding a sentence 'in the sense in which it can be replaced by another which says the same' (PI §531) will be called 'external' 'to mark the fact that what is grasped in it is, because "something common to different sentences", not understood as internal to any one specific formulation.'[17] Taken together, these two senses comprise the concept of understanding (PI §533) which can therefore be said to consist of both a paraphrasable and a non-paraphrasable aspect.[18]

We can now apply this distinction in order to understand what Wittgenstein means when he speaks of understanding religious utterances such as 'God's eye sees everything' or 'we might see one another after death' (LC 70). If what I have been arguing so far is correct, then, if I am to understand sentences of this kind, I must primarily understand them 'internally', as a purely 'external' understanding based on a grasp of what the individual words

---

[15] See Diamond, *op.cit.*, 128.
[16] Ridley, *op.cit.*, 32–3.
[17] *Ibid.*
[18] *Ibid.*, 26.

mean in ordinary contexts will not be sufficient to effect a real understanding of what is going on here. This is why Wittgenstein says: 'In one sense, I understand all he [the person who says he believes in a Judgement Day] says – the English words "God", "separate", etc. I understand. I could say: "I don't believe in this", and this would be true, meaning I haven't got these thoughts or anything that hangs together with them. But not that I could contradict the thing.' (LC 55)

What Wittgenstein seems to be saying here is that in order to be able to contradict a religious statement, you not only need to understand what the 'atoms' – i.e. the individual words – it is comprised of mean in ordinary contexts, but what the sentence as a whole means, and for this to be possible, you must understand how the words are functioning in *this* specific context – you must, that is, understand their technique of application *here* – something that cannot be accomplished by, for example, simply hazarding a guess about what the words composing the sentence might or might not be 'referring' to.[19] This is why Wittgenstein says that in one sense he understands all the religious person says, because he understands, for example, the ordinary words 'God' or 'separate',[20] but that, in another sense, he doesn't understand the sentence *at all* for, in this particular context, he has no grasp of how these familiar words are used: 'my normal technique of language leaves me' (LC 55).

Wittgenstein's case, to borrow an example of Diamond's, is similar to someone who understands the ordinary use of the word 'beautiful', say, but who is at a loss when someone applies it to a person like George Eliot, for example. For according to the habitual criteria George Eliot obviously isn't beautiful. If I am therefore to understand this new application of a familiar concept, my ordinary vision must, as it were, first be transformed. In Diamond's words:

> She [George Eliot], that magnificently ugly woman, gives a totally transformed meaning to 'beauty'. Beauty itself becomes something entirely new for one, as one comes to see (to one's

---

[19] See also Putnam, *op.cit.*, 165.

[20] It is unclear why Wittgenstein speaks of 'separate' in connection with a discussion of a Last Judgement, but I presume he is thinking of sentences such as 'the soul is separate from the body' or some such thing, but of course this is only a guess. What exactly Wittgenstein meant is irrelevant to our discussion, though.

own amazement, perhaps) a powerful beauty residing in this woman . . . In such a case, she is not judged by a norm available through the concept of beauty; she shows the concept up, she moves one to use the words 'beauty' and 'beautiful' almost as new words, or as renewed words. She gives one a new vocabulary, a new way of taking the world in in one's words, and of speaking about it to others.[21]

That is to say, a 'conceptual reorientation'[22] must take place if I am to understand the application of the word 'beautiful' to George Eliot – a reorientation which, as Diamond says, makes possible new ways of speaking about the world. And something similar, if Wittgenstein is right, happens in religious contexts, when I am, for instance, suddenly brought to understand, perhaps through certain kinds of experiences of dependence and dependability,[23] what it means to call God 'Father'. In this respect, just as George Eliot 'moves one to use the words "beauty" and "beautiful" almost as new words', so, it could be said, God moves the religious believer to use the words 'father' or 'fatherly love' almost as new words.

Consequently, one could now say that for someone for whom this 'conceptual reorientation' does not occur, no real understanding of the sentence (or words) in question is possible. That is to say, someone like Wittgenstein, who does not know what to make of the 'after death man's'[24] words, can be said only to 'understand' such sentences in the sense that he recognizes, for example, the ordinary English words 'scrutiny', 'soul' etc. that might comprise them, but without being able to understand, to speak with Diamond, the 'renewed use' of these words. This would be similar to someone who knows that the sun is a star located at the centre of our Solar System, but who fails to see the aptness of the phrase 'Juliet is the sun'.[25] And such a failure of understanding cannot be remedied by, say, pointing at Juliet and at the sun and saying, 'she is like that', but rather by drawing attention to aspects of the sun that make the comparison with Juliet meaning-

---

[21] Diamond, *op.cit.*, 125.
[22] *Ibid.*
[23] Compare Wittgenstein's talk of 'feeling absolutely safe' in the 'Lecture on Ethics'.
[24] This phrase is Diamond's.
[25] This example is Ridley's.

ful. If this still does not help, then perhaps getting the person to read more poetry might gradually make understanding dawn.[26]

It is ironic that in most philosophical domains, it is fairly commonplace nowadays to appeal to context and practice when it comes to the question of understanding something; indeed, as regards understanding ethical and aesthetic concepts, for example, one even speaks of cultivating certain virtues of character said to be necessary for making such understanding possible. But when it comes to understanding religious language, these lessons are generally forgotten and it is assumed that here the only pertinent question to ask is whether religious language 'refers'. As if there were only *one* thing referring could be, as if what constitutes 'referring' doesn't itself, in many ways, depend on *context* (and thus on the relevant practice) – noticing a 'religious fact', if one wants to talk that way, requires an understanding of theological concepts, such as, for example, seeing the point of calling God 'Father' – just as understanding a 'mathematical fact' needs the established practice of mathematics.[27]

So when Wittgenstein is, for example, saying that 'Christianity is not a doctrine, not, I mean, a theory about what has happened and will happen to the human soul, but a description of something that actually takes place in human life' (CV 28e), he is not suggesting that Christianity has no conceptual – no paraphrasable – content. Rather, what he means is that being able, say, to recite the Creeds or Catholic dogma is not sufficient for having any real understanding of religious concepts, as this requires being able to see religious utterances non-instrumentally, that is to say, it requires being able to see their *point* and aptness rather than their ability, as it were, to convey 'information' about God. And being able to see this is not possible, if Wittgenstein is right, independently of having some familiarity and grasp of the Christian form of life. Hence, when Wittgenstein says that the important thing with regard to the Christian 'doctrine' is to understand 'that you have to change your *life*' or 'the *direction* of your life' (CV 53e), he is not implying that it is somehow possible to do this *without* committing oneself to the Christian claims. For

---

[26] Of course it is possible that regardless of what one tries, understanding will never occur. In such cases one may want to speak, like Wittgenstein, of a kind of 'aspect blindness'.

[27] The circularity involved here is analogous to that of paraphrase presupposing itself and is therefore harmless.

to say that much more than rote-reciting is required, is not to say that therefore the 'doctrine' – the Christian claims – are irrelevant, as this would be as absurd as thinking that because a song can be sung both with and without expression, you could have the expression without the song (LC 29).

Consequently, it is simply not the case, as Nielsen assumes, that on the one hand we have the 'beliefs', on the other we have the 'practice' and, if we are very lucky, there are a handful of religious believers for whom the two come in a package. For it makes no sense to think that the 'beliefs' can be specified (in anything but a purely minimalist – 'external' – sense) completely independently of the practices in which they are embedded (and vice versa), just as it makes no sense to believe that 'the meaning or thought is just an accompaniment of the word' (*ibid.*), and word and thought, like 'belief' and 'practice', can therefore be divorced from each other.

This also helps us to understand what Wittgenstein means when he says that 'in religion every level of devoutness must have its appropriate form of expression which has no sense at a lower level. This doctrine, which means something at a higher level, is null and void for someone who is still at the lower level; he *can* only understand it *wrongly* and so these words are *not* valid for such a person.' (CV 32e) Here Wittgenstein is suggesting that there are different levels of understanding as regards religious statements corresponding to the relative depth of devoutness and spiritual development of the person concerned. So, for example, someone who thinks that the expression 'the Lord has given, the Lord has taken away, blessed be the name of the Lord' is a cheap attempt at trying to justify the caprice of the deity, is at a lower level of religious understanding than someone who sees it as a trusting acceptance of God's sovereignty. If the idea that spiritual development is necessary for a proper understanding of religious expressions to occur strikes us as implausible, it may again be useful to remind ourselves of what goes on in aesthetic contexts. Someone, for example, who lacks a musical education and does not possess a 'musical ear' will not be able to contradict the judgement of a connoisseur, as such a person will not have sufficient (musical) sensibility even really to understand what the connoisseur is saying. In other words, such a person will neither possess the vocabulary nor have the appropriate concepts that would enable them to say anything genuinely meaningful about a musical work, short, perhaps, of finding it 'pleasurable' or 'relaxing'. For exactly analogous reasons Wittgenstein feels that he cannot contradict what the religious person is saying, since he, as yet, lacks a real grasp of the concepts involved. That is to say, just as there is musical sensibility and tone-deafness (and, to be sure, much in between), there is also religious sensibility and blindness for religion, and neither musical nor religious sensibility is acquired by learning a set of theses, doctrines, by heart – about who the great composers were, about the laws of counterpoint or about transubstantiation – since this would only bring about an 'external', i.e. purely intellectual, understanding of the subject comparable to having learnt a code.[28] But what is required here is the kind of understanding that makes the musical work or the prayer, for example, *live* for me, not the kind that allows me to parrot a form of words. And such an understanding can only be brought about by immersing oneself in the culture or practice that has given rise to these phenomena. This is why Wittgenstein says in the *Lectures on Aesthetics*: 'In order to get clear about aesthetic words you have to describe ways of living.'(LC 11) If we understand that this is so in the case of aesthetics, it is only prejudice which prevents us from seeing that this applies in exactly the same way to religion. Hence Wittgenstein's remark that he could only utter the word 'Lord' with meaning, if he lived *completely* differently (CV 33e).

Consequently, *pace* Nielsen, there is nothing at all reductive about Wittgenstein's account of religious belief. Wittgenstein is not concerned with taking the 'content' out of religious claims and reducing it 'to merely living in a certain way'. Rather, what Wittgenstein is at pains to show is that – as is so often the case in philosophy – the either/or Nielsen is confronting us with is really a false dichotomy. For no such thing as a fully-fledged understanding of any domain of discourse is possible without both aspects of understanding being present, without, that is, both the 'external' and the 'internal' aspect being available to the 'understander'. Hence, it is simply not the case that we have to choose between a purely 'external' – that is to say 'doctrinal' – account of religious belief and a kind of arbitrary, 'mystical' commitment to living a certain kind of life, as both alternatives involve serious distortions: if we don't want to have a purely 'external', code-like understanding of religious beliefs – which is really no understanding at all –

[28] See also Ridley, *op.cit.*, 31.

then religious beliefs cannot be understood and specified independently of the mode of life that gives them sense. Conversely, if we do not want to have mere religious passion – a kind of 'internal' understanding without any 'external' aspect, something, I take it, that is either unintelligible or some bizarre sort of rapture – then religious feeling must be expressible within the Christian conceptual framework. To put it in a more Kantian way: external understanding without internal understanding is empty, internal understanding without external understanding is blind.

Hence, as with all ordinary (non-religious) cases of understanding, if a proper understanding of religious concepts is to be possible, both the 'external' and the 'internal' aspects of it are necessary. That is to say, although, as I have argued, the internal aspect is more important in religious (and aesthetic) contexts, it is not possible to have this on its own. Consequently, if Wittgenstein is right, there is no such thing as 'simply living in a certain way' as opposed to 'believing certain things' or, indeed, vice versa. *Genuine* beliefs can never be divorced from and understood completely independently of the difference they make in one's life, for there is no such thing as believing something *in vacuo* – without a context (or practice) – unless one thinks, like Smythies, that believing something is tantamount to holding a certain mental image before one's mind (and we've already seen that this is confused). Consequently, it is not the case, as Nielsen and others suppose, that Wittgenstein denies that religious people believe different things to non-religious people. What he *is* denying is that any sense can be made of what those beliefs *are* independently of the form of life (or practice) which gives them sense. For there is no such thing, nor could there be such a thing – in religion or elsewhere – as simply inspecting the words alone in order to find out whether they make sense or not.

And it is just this that – despite making claims to the contrary – Nielsen does when attempting to dismiss 'God-talk' as incoherent:

It is not . . . that I think that God is an object among objects, but I do think . . . that he must – in some very unclear sense – be taken to be a particular existent among existents though, of course, 'the king' among existents, and a very special and mysterious existent, but not an object, not a kind of object, not just a categorical or classificatory notion, but not a non-particular either. Though he is said to be infinite, he is also said to be a person, and these two elements when put together seem at least to yield a glaringly incoherent notion. He cannot be an object – a spatio-temporal entity but he is also a he – a funny kind of he to be sure – who is also said to be a person – again a funny kind of person – who is taken to be a person without a body: a purely *spiritual* being. This makes him out to be a 'peculiar reality' indeed. He gets to be even more peculiar when we are told he is an *infinite* person as well. But now language has really gone on a holiday.[29]

Nielsen is, in this passage, taking religious language crudely *au pied de la lettre*, since he is simply assuming that because I can understand what 'person' and 'infinite' mean in ordinary contexts, I am able to understand the religious expression 'God is infinite' – as if this were just a matter of combining the two linguistic 'atoms' 'person' and 'infinite' into a 'peculiar' complex. But if what I have been arguing is correct, such an idea just doesn't make any sense. For if it did, it would, among other things, spell doom for most other domains of discourse as well. For example, we should be just as much at a loss about how it is possible to apply emotive language to music, say. That is, if Nielsen's 'analysis' of 'God-talk' is anything to go by, we would be confronted by the following dilemma: either we understand sentences such as 'the string quartet is tearful' because it makes sense for sounds or bits of marks on a page to be sad – an analogue to Nielsen's strictly literal rendering of religious language – or such sentences are, as Nielsen is fond of emphasizing, purely 'symbolic', i.e. the 'tearful' is merely a fancy way of saying something like 'arousing feelings of sadness in most perceivers' – a correlate of Nielsen's claim that if religious language can't be construed literally, then it reduces to 'morality touched by emotion'.[30] But, although philosophers have at one time or another held such views,[31] Nielsen's dilemma is surely just as much of a false dichotomy as the one between 'practice' and 'belief' discussed (and dismissed) earlier. So, if we have, as Mulhall puts it, such a 'remarkably impoverished conception of the kinds of non-factual or non-descriptive uses of language . . . there might be',[32] then it

---

[29]   Nielsen and Phillips, *op.cit.*, 123.
[30]   *Ibid.*, 314 (for an expecially stark expression of this either/or).
[31]   See, for example, J. L. Mackie, *The Miracle of Theism* (Oxford: Oxford University Press, 1982), 219–22.
[32]   See Stephen Mulhall's critique in Nielsen and Phillips, *op.cit.*, 308.

should, of course, come as no surprise that, on such a conception, 'God-talk' – along with moral and aesthetic language – will turn out to be incoherent. Rather than celebrating this fact, however, Nielsen should offer an argument showing why his narrow conception of language which can see no alternative to a factual (metaphysical)/symbolic divide should be the only game in town. The odd claim to having followed 'the very logic of God-talk'[33] isn't sufficient here, for if I am right, this is precisely what Nielsen has *not* done.[34]

II

If what I have been arguing so far is correct, this disposes of Nielsen's first charge. By way of concluding, I shall therefore now briefly address his second criticism about 'incommensurability'. More specifically, I will endeavour to answer the question 'does anything I have said during the course of this paper imply that religious believers have a 'conceptual scheme' which is in some sense 'incommensurable' with that of the atheist'? Two responses to this question are possible, neither of which advances Nielsen's case. If we take 'incommensurable' to mean what Davidson means by it, namely, 'largely true but not translatable',[35] then the answer to this question is 'no', as any good Wittgensteinian would take Davidson's 'short line' on this issue: 'nothing, it may be said, could count as evidence that some form of activity could not be interpreted in our language that was not at the same time evidence that that form of activity was not speech behaviour.'[36] That is to say, given that I have argued that use of words in their non-paraphrasable sense is parasitic on words being generally paraphrasable, there can, *ex hypothesi*, be no *complete* failure of 'translation'. So, for example, I cannot explain what 'God's eye sees everything' means to someone who does not understand the

[33] Nielsen and Phillips, *op.cit.*, 123.
[34] Compare also Diamond's remark that talk of God having scattered his people 'no more depends on a metaphysical conception of how an incorporeal being can intervene in human history than does talk of Ford Motor Company as having acted [as when it was charged with manslaughter].' Diamond, *op.cit.*, 129.
[35] Donald Davidson, 'On the Very Idea of a Conceptual Scheme' in *Inquiries into Truth and Interpretation* (Oxford: Oxford University Press, 2001), 194. By 'not translatable' Davidson means 'not translatable *at all*'.
[36] Davidson, *op.cit.*, 185.

habitual senses of the words comprising the sentence. Neither, *pace* Nielsen, could I explain what 'eye' means in this context by pointing, say, to God's 'anatomy', since it is obvious that the word 'eye' in the sentence 'God's eye sees everything' does not function in the same way as the word 'eye' does in the sentence 'a racoon's eye can see in the dark'. It is equally obvious that I could not apply the word 'eye' to God, if I could not employ the word 'eye' in everyday contexts – if, that is, I could not understand 'a racoon's eye can see in the dark' and similar sentences. Religious discourse cannot, therefore, be 'self-contained' or 'sealed off' from other linguistic 'domains', for it is precisely the quotidian senses of words that make possible the 'renewed' uses or applications of these words in religious contexts. In this respect, religious discourse, like aesthetic language use, involves an *extension* or *transformation* of everyday discourse and consequently can't be 'incommensurable' with it.

If all we mean by 'incommensurable', however, is that there can be a partial 'translation failure' – in the sense that religious expressions are not instrumentally intersubstitutable – then the answer to our question is 'yes', but unsurprising and harmless. For such a 'translation failure' would be similar to a lyrical novel's (or poem's) resisting translation into another language. That is to say, although it can of course be done, what is distinctive about the poetic work will get 'lost in translation', something that will be apparent to anyone who ever tried to translate Proust's *A la Recherche du Temps Perdu* into English.

If this is correct, then Nielsen's bringing Davidson into the discussion at all is either irrelevant or merely a diversionary tactic (for, naturally, Davidson allows for partial translation failure[37]). Furthermore, given that Nielsen seems, in some sense, to regard

---

[37] Some philosophers, such as Hanjo Glock and including presumably Nielsen, read Davidson as not allowing for partial translation failure. I believe, although I cannot argue it in detail here, that such a reading is not borne out by the text. It would, for example, be hard to square with the following passage: 'A language may contain simple predicates whose extensions are matched by no simple predicates, or even by no predicates at all, in some other language. What enables us to make this point in particular cases is an ontology common to the two languages, with concepts that individuate the same objects. We can be clear about breakdowns in translation when they are local enough, for a background of generally successful translation provides what is needed to make these failures intelligible. But we were after larger game: we wanted to make sense of there being a language we could not translate at all.' (*op. cit.*, 192, see also my quotation in the main text below.) Be that as it may, if Davidson were nonetheless (and in spite of what he just seems to have said) committed to the view that partial translation failure is impossible, then his view is just false,

himself as a faithful disciple of Davidson's, it is ironic that he himself, in his criticisms of Wittgenstein's conception of religious belief, ends up espousing a version of the scheme/content distinction Davidson deplores. For Nielsen's first charge against Wittgenstein presupposes that it is possible to separate religious 'content' – the 'beliefs', the 'doctrine' – from the 'scheme' (the religious practice and life), but, if Davidson is right, then this is something we can't do:

> If we choose to translate some alien sentence rejected by its speakers by a sentence to which we are strongly attached on a community basis, we may be tempted to call this a difference in schemes; if we decide to accommodate the evidence in other ways, it may be more natural to speak of a difference of opinion. But when others think differently from us, no general principle, or appeal to evidence, can force us to decide that the difference lies in our beliefs rather than in our concepts.[38]

So when Nielsen says that 'individual practices and clusters of practices forming whole domains of discourse, such as science, religion or morality, can be criticized by reference to their fit with the forms of language/forms of life taken as a whole',[39] this sounds suspiciously like a linguistic version of what Davidson is rejecting – 'a neutral ground, or common co-ordinate system'[40] that we can appeal to when criticizing other practices (or 'schemes'). But, if that is so, then Nielsen just hasn't learnt Davidson's lesson.

Consequently, I can, of course, criticize other practices, including religious practices, but not by reference to their 'fit' or failure to 'fit' with the forms of life 'taken as a whole'.[41] For there is no such thing, nor could there be such a thing, as a form of life-in-general consisting of all our diverse practices taken together and

---

for we clearly get such translation failure all the time, which is, for example, why we employ German words like *Dasein* when translating Heidegger into English.

[38]   *Ibid.*, 197.

[39]   Kai Nielsen, *op.cit.*, 128.

[40]   Davidson, *op.cit.*, 198.

[41]   For example, one might, as Mulhall points out, share Nietzsche's suspicions of Christianity as embodying sado-masochistic self-hatred or Freud's suspicions of institutionalized religion as pandering to psychologically immature dependence on a father-figure ('Wittgenstein and Philosophy of Religion' in D. Z. Phillips and Timothy Tessin (eds), *Philosophy of Religion in the 21ˢᵗ Century* (New York: Palgrave, 2001), 106).

supplying us with a 'neutral set of criteria' against which individual practices can be measured and found wanting.[42] So, it seems that while Wittgenstein and Davidson are both at pains to dispose of the 'third dogma of empiricism', Nielsen – despite claiming to reject it too – is busily plotting its return.[43]

---

[42] Now if Nielsen's suggestion that religion can be judged against forms of language/ forms of life taken as a whole meant nothing more objectionable than that someone's religious beliefs should cohere with his/her views about the world generally, this would be a perfectly reasonable demand. Unfortunately, this is not the case. Nielsen is not concerned with the question of whether someone's religious beliefs might (or should) cohere with their other beliefs about the world, but rather seeks to distil a neutral set of criteria from all our practices taken together (whatever that could be) and then to employ this as a stick to beat religion with. That is to say, Nielsen wants to show that by the lights of this 'neutral set of criteria' religious beliefs can be found to be 'inherently incoherent.'

[43] This paper is based on material taken from my book *A Confusion of the Spheres – Kierkegaard and Wittgenstein on Philosophy and Religion* (Oxford: Oxford University Press, 2007). My thanks to the editor for permission to draw on this material here and to Aaron Ridley for comments on previous drafts.

5

THE TIGHTROPE WALKER

Severin Schroeder

Abstract
Contrary to a widespread interpretation, Wittgenstein did not regard credal statements as merely metaphorical expressions of an attitude towards life. He accepted that Christian faith involves belief in God's existence. At the same time he held that although as a hypothesis, God's existence is extremely implausible, Christian faith is not unreasonable. Is that a consistent view?

According to Wittgenstein, religious faith should not be seen as a hypothesis, based on evidence, but as grounded in a proto-religious attitude, a way of experiencing the world or certain aspects of it. A belief in religious metaphysics is not the basis of one's faith, but a mere epiphenomenon. Given further that religious doctrine is both falsification-transcendent and that religious faith is likely to have beneficial psychological effects, religious doctrine can be exempt from ordinary standards of epistemic support. An unsupported religious belief need not be unreasonable.

However, it is hard to see how one could *knowingly* have such an unsupported belief, as Wittgenstein seems to envisage. How can one believe what, at the same time, one believes is not likely to be true? This, I argue, is the unresolved tension in Wittgenstein's philosophy of religion.

The honest religious thinker is like a tightrope walker. It almost looks as though he were walking on nothing but air. His support is the slenderest imaginable. And yet it really is possible to walk on it. [CV 84]

I

Religious belief is widely thought to be irrational: a view about the world for which there is no reliable evidence and which can easily be explained as the product of upbringing, tradition uncritically accepted, and naive wishful thinking. Indeed it is not only ill-supported, there is reason to doubt whether its tenets ultimately make any sense. Its very consistency is threatened by a number of conceptual problems related to the notion of an omnipotent, omniscient and benevolent being. Wittgenstein would have agreed with this critical view: as an hypothesis to be assessed in cold blood in the light of its evidence and coherence theism is a lost cause. And yet he did not dismiss the belief in God as necessarily irrational. It may not be reasonable, but it need not be unreasonable either (LC 58). How is that possible? How can one be an 'honest religious thinker', in other words, how can one combine being a thinker – a rational person –, being honest – not deceiving oneself –, and being religious – believing in God. It is possible, according to Wittgenstein, but it is extremely difficult: a tightrope walk.

The problem, in short, is how to reconcile the following two statements held by Wittgenstein:

(1) As a hypothesis, God's existence (&c) is extremely implausible.
(2) Christian faith is not unreasonable.

To achieve this reconciliation it has been suggested that Christian faith according to Wittgenstein does not actually involve any metaphysical beliefs. Credal statements should be seen merely as figurative expressions of a certain attitude towards life, or as part of a ritualistic practice expressive of such an attitude.[1] But the obvious objection to such an expressivist construal of credal statements is that it is not a correct account of the actual religious language-game. Christian believers do not, on the whole, intend their credal statements to be taken in this merely figurative, expressivist sense. Thus it would appear that what Wittgenstein shows to be not unreasonable is not in fact Christian faith, but merely a carefully sanitized substitute, a demythologized version of the popular brew: with (nearly) the same emotional taste, but without its noxious metaphysical stimulants.

However, both the expressivist interpretation of Wittgenstein's position and the standard objection to it miss their target. First, Wittgenstein does not offer an account of '*the* religious language-game'. He is not offering an analysis of what people in general mean when they speak of God, the Resurrection or life after death. He was well aware how commonly people did take their

---

[1]   Phillips 1993.

beliefs about God to be something like metaphysical hypotheses. He repeatedly mentions examples of this more straightforward construal of religious beliefs (LC 57–9, OCD 159). He had a very low opinion of this kind of view, to be sure, but he was clearly not trying to deny that people (even intelligent people) had such beliefs.[2] He was not trying to tell such people that really when they used the word 'God' they were merely expressing a certain attitude towards life.[3]

What was Wittgenstein's intention then? He was trying to describe the kind of religious belief that he personally found appealing: comprehensible, intellectually respectable and morally attractive. The kind of faith, in fact, that he would have liked to have; that he so often felt in need of; without ever being able to attain it. (It is worth remembering the rather private nature of what we have of Wittgenstein's remarks on religion. The only remarks on the topic that can be attributed to him verbatim – and probably the most illuminating ones – are private diary entries, never intended for publication.)[4] So even *if* Wittgenstein's

[2] Of Yorick Smythies and Elizabeth Anscombe, who were both Roman Catholics, he said: 'I could not possibly bring myself to believe all the things that they believe' (M 60); OC §336; B 34f.

[3] Note that the situation is very different here from what it is in other areas where Wittgenstein did indeed contradict people's own accounts of what their words meant. For example, mathematicians may be firmly convinced that in using numbers they are talking about Platonic entities. That can be set aside because it can be made plausible that such metaphysical interpretations are irrelevant to the everyday use of number signs. When a philosopher of mathematics says that he believes that the equation '$10 - 3 = 7$' describes eternal relations between abstract objects, one may reply: 'You can believe these things if you like, but that has very little to do with their actual use in our language. It is not part of your arithmetic competence. What matters is, for example, that if I owe you 3 pounds and give you 10 pounds you have to give me 7 pounds change. That is an example of what constitutes the public meaning of those expressions in our language. And as far as that is concerned, the linguistic meaning of those signs, your metaphysical beliefs are irrelevant.' However, no such move can be made plausible in the case of credal statements. For they are expressly about what metaphysical beliefs people hold, and so those beliefs cannot be set aside as irrelevant. Rather, what people say here is (on Wittgenstein's view) protected by first-person authority. I cannot be mistaken in my honest expression of my beliefs (which covers even inconsistencies as long as they are not too obvious).

[4] Many of them were posthumously published under the title *Vermischte Bemerkungen* or, in English translation as *Culture and Value*. The text of the 'Lectures on Religious Belief' is doubly unreliable: For one thing, the students writing those notes may have misunderstood or misremembered what Wittgenstein said. For another thing, what Wittgenstein said in those improvised and informal classes may well have been tentative or carelessly phrased. Once in a lecture on aesthetics, given at about the same time, he stopped a student from taking notes saying: 'If you write these spontaneous remarks down, some day someone may publish them as my considered opinions. I don't want that done. For I am talking now freely as my ideas come, but all this will need a lot more thought and better expression'

remarks could indeed be read as a downright expressivist account of religious statements, the common objection that he misdescribed ordinary believers' religious views would be mistaken. Wittgenstein was not concerned with ordinary believers' religious views. He was interested only in an approach to religion that appealed to him personally – however uncommon or even idiosyncratic that approach might be. By contrast, certain other types of belief in the supernatural, however prevalent among, or even characteristic of, common-or-garden Christians, Wittgenstein regarded as contemptuously as did Nietzsche, Freud or Russell: as wholly irrational, indeed as forms of superstition (LC 59).

Secondly, contrary to that widespread view, Wittgenstein did not propound a purely expressivist construal of credal statements. At first glance, a form of expressivism – the reduction of religious belief to an attitude towards life – seems to be suggested by the following passage written in 1947:[5]

> It appears to me as though a religious belief could only be (something like) passionately committing oneself to a system of coordinates // a system of reference. [CV 73]

However, the expression 'could only be' is just another way of saying 'must be'; it does *not* mean 'is only' or 'is nothing but'. For instance: 'The thief could only be a member of staff' does not mean: 'The thief is nothing but a member of staff'. Clearly, the person in question will be other things as well, in particular – a thief. Similarly, the claim that a religious belief can only be (i.e. must be) a passionate commitment is not supposed to rule out that it is not also a belief. And that is exactly what Wittgenstein says expressly in the sentence immediately following:

> Hence although it is *belief*, it is a way of living, or a way of judging life. [CV 73]

Thus, Wittgenstein stresses the importance of commitment, the practical dimension of religious faith, without denying that it is, or involves, also *believing* certain things to be true.[6]

(OCD 141). Obviously the same applies to the notes M. O'C. Drury and Norman Malcolm published of their conversations with Wittgenstein.

[5]   Cf. Hyman 2001, 5–7.

[6]   It should also be noted that the German word '*Glaube*' covers both belief and faith. Thus some of Wittgenstein's remarks about religious 'belief' may be better translated as about faith.

This becomes perfectly clear when he notes and deplores his own lack of faith. He was very sympathetic towards the Christian faith, but ultimately he felt unable to embrace it himself – because he could not bring himself to *believe* what Christians believe.

> I cannot call [Jesus] *Lord*; because that says absolutely nothing to me. . . . I cannot utter the word "Lord" meaningfully. *Because I do not believe* that he will come to judge me [CV 38].

A little later in the same passage he explains why it is essential for a Christian to believe in Christ's resurrection:

> If he did not rise from the dead, then he decomposed in the grave like every human being . . . & can no longer *help*; & we are once more orphaned & alone. [CV 38][7]

And he adds: 'Only *love* can believe the Resurrection' (CV 39).[8] Far from denying people's belief in the supernatural, he is trying here to explain its psychology.

Christian faith, for Wittgenstein, involves the belief in 'redemption through Christ's death' (D 193) and also the belief in 'eternal life & eternal punishment' (D 188); neither of which he himself has (D 190; 1937). Again, in a passage written in 1944 he characterises a miracle as 'a gesture which God makes' and adds: 'Now, do I believe that this happens? I don't' (CV 51).[9] And in his 1938 lectures he expressly rejects the reductivist suggestion that a statement about life after death is merely an expression of 'a certain attitude': 'No', he responds. 'It says what it says. Why should you be able to substitute anything else?' (LC 71).

The fact that, contrary to what is commonly said, Wittgenstein did not mean to reduce credal statements to metaphorical expressions of an attitude towards life bars the easy way of reconciling propositions (1) and (2). So the question is how, according to Wittgenstein, one could reconcile:

> (1) As a hypothesis, God's existence (&c) is extremely implausible.

---

[7]   Cf. I Cor. 15:17.
[8]   Cf.: '[Someone says:] ". . . there will be a Resurrection of you." If some said: "Wittgenstein, do you believe in this?" I'd say: "No." ' (LC 53)
[9]   Cf. E 16. 1. 1918; 21. 6. 1920.

(2) Christian faith is not unreasonable.

(3) Christian faith does involve belief in God's existence (&c).

II

Religious faith has both a theoretical or intellectual and an emotional-practical side. On the theoretical side there are certain historical and cosmological beliefs, on the other side there are certain rituals, observances, typical responses and forms of behaviour, and moral and emotional attitudes. What, according to Wittgenstein, is the relationship between those two irreducible aspects of religion: between, in particular, doctrinal beliefs and emotional attitudes?

It is important to note that the mundane model of evidence, belief and attitude is not satisfactorily applicable to the religious case. Ordinarily, there is a justificatory chain of three parts:

$$\text{evidence } -[justifies]{\rightarrow}\text{belief } -[justifies]{\rightarrow}\text{attitude}$$

For instance, I have been bitten by my neighbour's dog before; therefore I believe that dog to be dangerous; therefore I am afraid of the dog and inclined to avoid it. Similarly, it is often thought that the world provides evidence for God's existence and that the Gospels provide evidence of God's incarnation in Jesus of Nazareth who worked miracles, was crucified and raised from the dead. Then the belief in God and Jesus Christ provides a reason for a Christian attitude towards life. However, since Hume it has often and persuasively been argued that the evidence for the truth of Christian doctrine is grossly insufficient.[10] Moreover, even the second step: from a theoretical belief in the cosmological and historical tenets of Christian doctrine to a Christian attitude, is problematic. Suppose there is an omnipotent being who created the world, visited the world in a human body, worked miracles and was crucified; suppose further that those who believe in him and submit to him will be rewarded after death and those who don't will be punished. Such a belief will of course yield a *prudential* reason to become a Christian; just as those living in a totalitarian

---

[10]   The critical arguments are well known. For the purpose of this paper, I assume them, or some of them, to be by and large successful. For a useful survey see Mackie 1982.

country have a prudential reason to show approval of their dictator. But it is difficult to see, in either case, how such a situation should engender *love* for the ruler (cf. CV 92f.). Of course Christians will urge that God loves us, and therefore deserves to be loved by us. The problem is that His love does not seem to be obvious: not in His wish to be worshipped by His creatures (John 4:23) and His condemning of those who don't believe in Him (John 3:18), and not in the world of toil and suffering he has created (cf. CV 34), even if one takes into account the possible compensations of an afterlife. This is the well-known problem of evil. As a solution it has been suggested (by Leibniz and others) that with all its misery this world is still the best of all possible worlds: that there is a *logical* link between happiness, freedom and suffering such that even an omnipotent god could not have created a better world.[11] The weakness of this defence is that no such logical link has actually been demonstrated. So the defence doesn't show that the evidence against a benevolent god *is* deceptive, it merely shows that it is conceivable that it *might be* deceptive. But that is true of all empirical evidence and does not undermine the evidence. Things are different, however, if the belief in God is not based on empirical evidence in the first place. In that case, if one is independently certain of God's existence, a reassurance that it may not be logically inconsistent with the world's misery could indeed be found sufficient. There is a great difference between somebody who already 'knows' that God is good and only needs to reconcile that with the state of the world and somebody who tries to work out from the evidence of the world whether there is a benevolent god. For the former it may well be appropriate to say that 'the ways of the Lord are unfathomable', for the latter such a response will not do.[12]

Wittgenstein agrees with many philosophical critics of religion that belief in religious doctrine cannot rationally be based on any empirical evidence.[13] A belief that could be established on evidence would not be religious:

---

[11] Cf. Cottingham 2005, 26–36.
[12] To use a distinction by Gabriel Marcel, the believer may regard the amount of evil and suffering in the world as a *mystery*, whereas the sceptic must see it as a *problem* (cf. Cottingham 2005, 159f.).
[13] The attempt to show religious belief to be reasonable in the light of the evidence struck Wittgenstein as 'ludicrous' (LC 58).

The point is that if there were evidence, this would in fact destroy the whole business [LC 56].

This idea can be developed by a thought experiment:

We come to an island and we find beliefs there, and certain beliefs we are inclined to call religious. [LC 58]

The islanders may, for example, believe that there is an immensely powerful being that can punish them or reward them, and that they worship. But now suppose they take us to the peak of a mountain where indeed we see that powerful being: somebody who sometimes strikes people dead and sometimes cures people's illnesses by a touch of the hand. Then we will no longer call their attitude towards that being a religious belief (cf. LC 60); it has turned out to be a straightforward piece of knowledge of, and a reasonable response of awe and submission to, a superior person.

III

Having rejected the mundane evidence-belief-attitude model as inappropriate to religious belief, Wittgenstein invites us to turn things round and regard a religious, or proto-religious, attitude, a way of experiencing the world or certain aspects of it, as basic and of primary importance. Such an attitude or cluster of feelings is not a mere consequence of a theoretical belief, it is the very root and centre of faith. Here are a few examples:

(i) In the *Tractatus* Wittgenstein writes:

6.44 It is not *how* things are in the world that is mystical, but *that* it exists.

Later, in a lecture (1929), he elaborates this thought. He speaks of a particular experience that makes him '*wonder at the existence of the world*' (LE 41; cf. WVC 118). Such a feeling 'of seeing the world as a miracle' (LE 43) may well give rise to, and become contained in, the idea of a supernatural creation of the world, of God as the creator (LE 42).

(ii) In the same lecture he mentions another proto-religious experience: 'the experience of feeling *absolutely* safe' (LE 41; cf.

WVC 68). Norman Malcolm remembered how Wittgenstein told him of his first encounter with this idea:

> He told me that in his youth he had been contemptuous of [religion], but that at about the age of twenty-one something had caused a change in him. In Vienna he saw a play that was mediocre drama, but in it one of the characters expressed the thought that no matter what happened in the world, nothing bad could happen to *him* – *he* was independent of fate and circumstance. Wittgenstein was struck by this stoic thought; for the first time he saw the possibility of religion. [M 58]

Obviously, there is no such thing as absolute safety from diseases, accidents or crimes, but one can have a feeling that somehow these things don't matter; that whatever happens, in some strange sense it will be all right. From such a feeling of absolute safety it is but a short step to feeling safe in the hands of God (LE 42). This emotion is essential to Wittgenstein's conception of religion: 'Religious faith . . . is a trusting' (CV 82). Thanks to this basic trust, '[f]or a truly religious man nothing is tragic' (OCD 107; cf. CV 21d). The religious temperament that Wittgenstein had in mind is able to accept everything in the world with equanimity, a peaceful resignation that can find expression in the words 'It was God's will' (CV 69f.). It is not that one first understands theoretically and on reliable evidence that God is a firm protection against all possible dangers and consequently one feels safe; rather, it is the other way round. A basic feeling of safety, an indomitable disposition to trust and hope may lead to the idea of divine protection.

(iii) Many people are naturally inclined to be grateful for the happiness they experience. Where life is felt to be beautiful, a blessing, a gift, one can easily be moved to form the idea of a giver whom one would like to praise and thank (cf. Cottingham 2006, §4). If, on the other hand, one is deeply impressed by the dark side of life – the incessant toil, suffering, atrocities and futility – one may, like Schopenhauer, feel the opposite inclination: of looking for somebody to blame or be indignant about, if not a devilish creator, at least a ubiquitous world will.

(iv) An acute conscience brings ideas of right and wrong and their sanctions to the forefront of a person's mind:

> One person might, for instance, be inclined to take everything that happened to him as a reward or punishment . . . If he is ill,

he may think: "What have I done to deserve this?" . . . [Or] he thinks in a general way whenever he is ashamed of himself: "This will be punished." [LC 54f.]

This inclination will naturally lead to the idea of a superhuman judge, who sees everything, and of a final reckoning. At the same time, the stern sense of duty that tends to accompany such a moralizing view of life may produce thoughts of eternal existence:

Wittgenstein once suggested that a way in which the notion of immortality can acquire a meaning is through one's feeling that one has duties from which one cannot be released, even by death. [M 59; cf. LC 70]

In a similar vein he once remarked to Drury:

If what we do now is to make no difference in the end, then all the seriousness of life is done away with. [OCD 161]

Hence if you are, in Wittgenstein's demanding sense, serious about life, you may feel that life cannot be as transitory as it appears; somehow there must be more to come.

(v) An uncommonly severe conscience may make it impossible for a person ever to be satisfied with himself. He will feel sinful and miserable, what William James called a 'sick soul' (1902, Lectures VI-VII). Bunyan was an example, Wittgenstein himself was another one. The sick soul is so desperate that nothing in the world can help – only a God. To Malcolm Wittgenstein once remarked

that he thought that he could understand the conception of God, in so far as it is involved in one's awareness of one's own sin and guilt. . . . I think [Malcolm adds] that the idea of Divine judgement, forgiveness, and redemption had some intelligibility for him, as being related in his mind to feelings of disgust with himself, an intense desire for purity, and a sense of the helplessness of human beings to make themselves better. [M 59]

In about 1944 Wittgenstein wrote:

People are religious to the extent that they believe themselves not so much *imperfect* as *sick*.

Anyone who is half-way decent will think himself utterly imperfect, but the religious person thinks himself *wretched*. [CV 51]

And a little later:

The Christian religion is only for the one who needs infinite help, that is, only for the one who suffers infinite distress. . . . Christian faith – so I believe – is refuge in this *ultimate* distress. [CV 52; cf. OCD 100]

Thus a certain type of moral despair can make someone experience the need for supernatural help, for a redeeming god. In another diary entry Wittgenstein insists that if Jesus is to be the redeemer he must be God: 'For a human being cannot redeem you' (D 145).

(vi) Lev Tolstoy, who at about the age of fifty was suddenly overwhelmed by an intense sense of the futility of life, a paralysing experience of a lack of meaning in life, is another type of the sick soul. Again, despair becomes so acute that the only possible cure can come from God. 'God', in this case, is the name of what could endow the world with the meaning the absence of which is so painfully felt.

Of course such religious or proto-religious emotions and attitudes are not in themselves religious belief (cf. LC 55b). They may bring with them, or manifest themselves in, a preoccupation with the idea of God, but they do not necessarily lead to a belief in the existence of God. One can feel drawn to those pictures, but never see more in them than pictures: metaphors, mythological expressions of one's feelings. That was Wittgenstein's case. He noted that he felt an 'inclination' towards belief in Christ's resurrection: 'I play as it were with the thought' (CV 38); but as far as we know he never actually believed in it.

But others did and do. Sometimes the further step is taken: a certain emotional attitude not only expresses itself in religious pictures and ideas, but those pictures and ideas are also believed to be literally true.

IV

The following six theses are an attempt to summarize Wittgenstein's picture of religious faith. Again, it needs to be stressed that

Wittgenstein was concerned only with the type of faith he found appealing; he was not interested in describing all possible forms of religious belief, or the essence of religious belief. Having read William James's *Varieties of Religious Experience*, he was aware 'that religion takes many forms, there are similarities, but there is nothing common among all religions' (B 55).[14]

1. A belief in religious metaphysics is a manifestation of a certain emotional or moral attitude.
2. A belief in religious metaphysics cannot be fully understood independently of the underlying attitude.
3. A belief in religious metaphysics is not the basis of one's faith, but a mere epiphenomenon.
4. Religious doctrine is falsification-transcendent.
5. Religious faith is likely to have an enormous beneficial impact on one's life.
6. Therefore (3, 4 & 5) religious doctrine can be exempt from ordinary standards of epistemic support.

I shall comment on these points in turn.

1. *A belief in religious metaphysics is a manifestation of a certain emotional or moral attitude.* Belief statements are not simply and directly expressions of an attitude (as R. B. Braithwaite suggested); they do indeed express a belief. However, that belief can itself be seen as a manifestation of a certain attitude. When Madeline Bassett declares that the stars are God's daisy chain and that whenever someone weeps a fairy dies, she may well be taken to believe these things. But her doing so characterises her. As Bertie might put it, she is just the kind of soppy girl that believes that sort of rot. Again, when an inveterate pessimist says 'I'm sure it will rain tomorrow and the picnic will be spoilt', this may be a sincere expression of what he believes, but at the same time it manifests his lugubrious temperament.

2. *A belief in religious metaphysics cannot be fully understood independently of the underlying attitude.* The attitude is 'part of the substance of the belief' (LC 56). Thus, Wittgenstein claims, the declaration that one believes in a Judgement Day may mean different things

---

[14] Indeed, James's warning 'that we may very likely find no one essence, but many characters which may alternately be equally important in religion' (James 26) was probably one of the inspirations for Wittgenstein's account of a family resemblance concept (PI §§65–75).

(LC 58), depending on what role it plays in one's feelings and one's life. More clearly, a person's belief in the Christian God may be a very different belief, depending on whether it is emotionally driven by ideas of sin and judgement (iv & v), or by exuberant feelings of love and gratitude (iii).

The attitude underpinning a belief can also be said to show in what is taken to establish the belief. 'The idea is given by what we call the proof' (LC 70). If the belief in immortality is taken to be established by the moral considerations mentioned above (iv): as a consequence of moral seriousness, then that tells us something about what kind of belief it is. It shows how different it is, for example, from the guarded acceptance of a scientific hypothesis supported by some provisional experimental evidence. Or if a Christian (of the kind Wittgenstein could respect) does not subject the Gospels to the same historical criticism as other reports from that time (cf. CV 37f.; OCD 101), his belief in the ministry and resurrection of Jesus can be seen to be different in kind from the beliefs he holds about the lives of Roman Emperors (LC 57). Then to criticise his idea of Jesus from a historical point of view would be a misunderstanding comparable to that of responding in all seriousness to a humorous suggestion, or of answering a hyperbolical statement with a pedantic demonstration that it is exaggerated.

When Mr Jarndyce (in *Bleak House*) feels vexed about the turn a conversation takes, he puts his discomfort down to easterly winds. If someone unfamiliar with Mr Jarndyce's ways were to notice that the wind was not in fact easterly and were to contradict him, the two would be at cross purposes. Although, we may assume, Mr Jarndyce does indeed believe that the wind is in the east on such an occasion (his complaint is not merely an eccentric figure of speech), it is not meant as an ordinary hypothesis about the weather. Strangely enough, Mr Jarndyce takes himself to have something like first-person authority about easterly winds. The way he uses the statement, he allows virtually no room for empirical confirmation or disconfirmation. That shows that what really matters in this case is the emotion of mental discomfort from which his meteorological belief springs and which is, as it were, the main substance of his belief.

Here we re-encounter the famous, or notorious, verification principle: not, however, in its crude polemical application to dismiss what is unverifiable as nonsense, but quite irenically employed as a means of distinguishing different types of proposition. Once in conversation Wittgenstein compared the question of verification to a policeman's enquiry about people's employment: A negative answer should also be envisaged and treated as a useful piece of information (M 55).

3. *A belief in religious metaphysics is not the basis of one's faith,* but only, as it were, its pediment or frieze decoration, *a mere epiphenomenon,* in itself comparatively unimportant (cf. CV 97). Not quite as unimportant, to be sure, as Mr Jarndyce's belief about the direction of the wind: For easterly wind is just one of countless possible causes of discomfort that could be named – among them of course the real concern that Mr Jarndyce is reluctant to consider –, whereas the link between the emotional attitudes described above and the accompanying creed is much more specific and understandable – and the religious belief is, arguably, not just a smoke screen to hide a person's real concern. Still, the details of a belief in religious metaphysics are underdetermined by the underlying emotional attitude. It may be important for a religious temperament to find *some* such belief for the underlying emotional attitude to 'make sense', to be rationalized (for example, one may feel compelled to believe in some addressee for one's feelings of gratitude); but this belief may take very different forms in different cultural settings.

In another sense, however, the details of the religious stories and dogmas may become very important. That is, although other stories and pictures might have done the same service, now that we have these they have through a venerable tradition become sacred to us. Religious doctrine tends to be treated in a ritualistic way, as something sacred that – however arbitrary in its origins – once established, must be observed and preserved unchanged. Wittgenstein thought that ritual was essential to religion (B 34) and disapproved strongly of breaks with religious tradition (e.g., the use of a piano, rather than an organ in church: OCD 121). Thus the details of the Gospel narrative, even their archaic diction, have become an integral part of the Christian ritual.[15]

Wittgenstein was also sensitive to the aesthetic attractions of religious doctrine. He found the symbolism of Christianity 'wonderful beyond words' (OCD 86), and hence, again, not easily replaceable by anything else. In a lecture Wittgenstein suggested the analogy that chess could also be played in writing, or with

---

[15] Cf.: 'a belief . . . can itself be ritualistic or part of a rite' (GB 129).

numbered cards instead of wooden pieces placed on the board
(e.g., '1' for a pawn, '2' for a knight &c.). But it may be very
important to our enjoyment of the game that it looks a bit like a
miniature battle (LC 72). Similarly, the Gospel narratives in all
their colourful details are not strictly necessary to codify the
crucial ideas of Christian doctrine (sin, and redemption through
God's incarnation, death and resurrection), but they obviously
add to its appeal.

The epiphenomenal character of the belief in religious metaphysics is probably what Wittgenstein has in mind when in his
lectures – in what must be a rhetorical overstatement – he denies
that there is a contradiction between theist and atheist (LC 53,
55). The case may be compared to that of a disagreement between
a music lover praising a piece in superlative terms and a tone-deaf
philistine who finds nothing worthwhile in it. On the face of it,
they do of course contradict each other ('This is wonderful!' 'No,
it isn't.'), but at a deeper level it is not so much that they disagree,
rather they cannot communicate at all. It is not that the tone-deaf
person knows what a truly wonderful piece of music is, but does
not think that this is one. Rather, he has no notion of wonderful
music. He has never had such an aesthetic experience. In such a
case the word 'contradiction' would over-intellectualize the disagreement and make it appear too slight. Similarly in the religious
case. What really matters, for Wittgenstein, is the emotional
underpinning. And on that level the opposition is not one
between holding true and holding false, but between having a
certain attitude and not having it.

4. *Religious doctrine is falsification-transcendent.* In the *Tractatus*
Wittgenstein remarked that 'God does not reveal himself *in* the
world' (TLP 6.432), and on this point he never changed his mind.
On the face of it, this of course appears to contradict directly what
any Christian will say. After all, God created the world, He lived
and died in the world as Jesus of Nazareth, and many people claim
that He answered their prayers and made Himself known to them.
However, none of this could ever be proved or disproved by those
who do not believe it. Religious belief is such that it will never be
in conflict with any possible experience. Those who feel safe in
the hands of God do not mean that they could not come to any
bodily harm (see III. (ii) above). God is believed to love us, but
nothing is thought to follow from this about the future course of
events. If a human being loves you, he will if he can protect you
from suffering; God's love, by contrast, is not expected to protect

Christians from suffering in this world, even though He is omnipotent. In an important sense belief in God is a *no-risk belief*. As, unlike ordinary beliefs (e.g. about other people's benevolence), it does not imply that anything particular will happen, it cannot be disappointed and one does not risk getting into trouble as a result. Therefore in everyday life – in earning their living and making provisions for their old age and their family – Christians do not because of their belief in God behave differently from other people.

It may be objected that Christianity is committed to the truth of certain historical claims that are, in principle, susceptible of confirmation or disconfirmation. Wittgenstein dismissed that as irrelevant:

> Queer as it sounds: the historical accounts of the Gospels might, in the historical sense, be demonstrably false, & yet belief [faith] would lose nothing through this: but *not* because it has to do with 'universal truths of reason'! rather, because historical proof (the historical proof-game) is irrelevant to belief [faith]. [CV 37f.]

Of course one cannot *accept* the Gospels to be demonstrably false (in their essential points, not only in details) and still believe them to be true. The point is rather that what in the research of ancient history is regarded as good evidence or even as proof is only ever of a certain probability, clearly not infallible, and can easily be overruled by the deeply felt certainty of faith. After all, a Christian believes that Jesus worked miracles and was resurrected from the dead; yet if one's belief is not restrained by the laws of nature, why should it be embarrassed by the mere probabilities of historical evidence?

5. *Religious faith is likely to have an enormous beneficial impact on one's life.* Analytic philosophy has seen religion predominantly as an intellectual challenge. Reasons for and against the existence of God have been discussed like reasons for and against the existence of qualia. Wittgenstein, by contrast, regarded religious faith above all as a powerful moral and psychological remedy (OCD 100). His own life was full of despair, he lived through a number of intense crises when time and again he was close to suicide. And he knew that his wretchedness and despair, the disgust he felt with what he regarded as his own sinfulness and vanity, was of the kind that others had overcome by a conversion to faith. He understood

very well how one could feel the need for religion: how the burden of one's sinfulness could become too heavy for one to carry, so that one could be redeemed only by God. He often felt a longing to 'be submerged in religion' (CV 54), but, alas, his knees wouldn't bend (CV 63).

The psychological efficacy of faith is beyond doubt. One hears frequently of people who have found solace in religion or who have been sustained by it to show great courage and moral integrity, and most of us have probably encountered confirmed believers whose friendly equanimity seems to testify to the beneficial moral and psychological effects of their faith.[16]

6. *Therefore (3, 4 & 5) religious doctrine can be exempt from ordinary standards of epistemic support.* To be rational is to do what is appropriate in the light of one's aims and objectives. In general, to be well-informed is likely to be useful in the pursuit of one's goals, to be misinformed is likely to be a hindrance to success. Therefore, it is rational to be critical. Credulity, a lack of care about the correctness of one's beliefs is, in general, irrational. But there are exceptions. For one thing, there may be areas of belief so far removed from anything we need to know in order to pursue our goals efficiently that an error is of no consequence. And for another thing, in some cases, the drawback of being misled by a false belief is outweighed by its beneficial psychological effects. Thus it may be better for a person not to learn a truth that would throw him into utter despair and ruin his life. And it is a psychological commonplace that optimism, a firm belief in one's own abilities and luck – even if it is unfounded –, tends to increase one's chances of success. Now, the argument is that religious doctrines are an area where credulity is not as irrational as it is elsewhere for both those reasons: because a possible error in the relevant metaphysical and historical beliefs will not mislead us in the pursuit of our mundane aims, and because holding those beliefs is likely to have considerable psychological benefits. At best, faith is a powerful medicine for overcoming despair, making contented, and facilitating moral improvement, at worst, it has no harmful side-effects since religious belief, cleared from superstition, in no way

---

[16] Of course there is also a lot to be said about the harmful effects of religious belief, from crusades to suicide bombers, but following Wittgenstein my concern in this paper is only with the possibility of a thoroughly attractive version of faith.

conflicts with everyday rationality. 'Go on,' Wittgenstein encourages himself in a diary entry, 'believe! It does no harm' (CV 52).

V

The problem is of course that one cannot simply decide what to believe. One can sometimes bring oneself to believe something, yet not by a mere act of the will, but by finding reasons or, at least, the impression that there are reasons. These, however, must be reasons to think the belief true (as believing is believing to be true), not just the expectation that having the belief would make one feel better. Of course, indirectly it *is* possible voluntarily to acquire or preserve beliefs because they are agreeable, or to prevent oneself from acquiring beliefs because they are disagreeable. This is done by avoiding exposure to what one suspects might be evidence or reasons for an undesirable belief. It is typically a matter of not pursuing matters as far as one could, not paying attention to what on closer inspection might undermine one's cherished views, and refraining from critical questions. Thus a husband in order to preserve his belief in his wife's faithfulness may decide to refrain from reading a suspicious looking letter that fell out of her handbag or not question her in too much detail about her doings during his absence. Similarly, somebody brought up in a Christian faith may at a later age be careful not to subject its tenets to any critical probing. Initiating a religious belief in such a way is much more difficult, but could perhaps be achieved by keeping company for a while exclusively with particularly friendly, admirable and eloquent adherents of that belief.

That is what is called self-deception. However conducive to one's happiness, for Wittgenstein it was out of the question. His ideal was the honest religious thinker, who is, and remains, fully aware that the arguments of natural theology are unconvincing. Even in the midst of his struggles to find some faith and overcome his misery Wittgenstein would exhort himself in his diary not to compromise his intellectual integrity: 'Let me . . . at all events not be superstitious!! *I don't want to be uncleanly in my thinking!* . . . Preserve my understanding pure and untainted!' (D 173f.).

If it is not possible to *bring* oneself into a state of religious belief without muddled thinking or self-deception, it may still be possible for some to *be* in that state. Perhaps some people are able to believe in God and resurrection even though they are fully aware that their belief has no rational basis. As Wittgenstein described it:

> redeeming love believes even in the Resurrection; . . . What fights doubt is *as it were redemption* . . . first be redeemed & hold on tightly to your redemption . . . – then you will see that what you are holding on to is this belief. [CV 39]

An intense religious emotion, answering and dissolving the despair of the sick soul (see III. (v) above), an overwhelming experience of feeling oneself forgiven and redeemed, is to bring with it a belief that needs no reasons: a belief that can be sustained solely by an emotion. Others have claimed that aesthetic considerations, experiences of beauty – in ritual and symbolism (cf. OCD 86, 93) – sustained their belief:

> 'But my dear Sebastian, you can't seriously *believe* it all.'
> 'Can't I?'
> 'I mean about Christmas and the star and the three kings and the ox and the ass.'
> 'Oh yes, I believe that. It's a lovely idea.'
> 'But you can't *believe* things because they're a lovely idea.'
> 'But I *do*. That's how I believe.'
> [Evelyn Waugh, *Brideshead Revisited*, ch. IV]

It may well be possible for an emotion to cause and sustain a belief, the question however remains whether it is compatible with the intellectual clarity Wittgenstein would not want to compromise. Can one believe with a clear awareness that one's belief is epistemically unsupported? Will a thinking person not feel compelled to find at least a semblance of a reason to make the belief appear respectable?

It may be useful to consider the analogy with optimism, which like religious belief may or may not be supported by reasons:

> Wittgenstein remarked that when someone said he was optimistic *because* the law of historical development showed that things were bound to get better, this was nothing he could admire. 'On the other hand, if someone says: "By the look of them, things are getting worse, and I can find no evidence to suggest

that they will improve. And yet in *spite* of this, I believe things will get better!" – I can admire that.' (RR 201f.)

The person who claims to give a rational justification for his optimism must be fooling himself. There is no law of historical development on which any optimism could be based. This is just bad reasoning, comparable perhaps to philosophers' well-known unconvincing attempts to prove the existence of God. Contrasted with that is the person whose belief in a better future is not claimed to be based on any dubious reasoning, but acknowledged to be the unjustified attitude of a sanguine temperament. Wittgenstein admires the latter person because he is honest and not guilty of bad reasoning. The first person's optimism is in all likelihood also the expression of a sanguine temperament, but, somewhat disingenuously, he prefers to dress it up as the result of some sophisticated reasoning. As F. H. Bradley put it, metaphysics is the finding of bad reasons for what we believe upon instinct.

However, the second person's stance is not free from difficulties. Changing the scenario a little, let us consider the simpler case of a seriously ill relative: the symptoms make it reasonable to expect the worst. Of course one can *expect* the worst and still keep up one's *hope* for a good outcome. Hope requires only a possibility, be it ever so slight, of what is hoped for, not probability. But suppose a person's temperament is indomitably optimistic to such a degree that he is not only always full of hope, but even feels compelled to *believe* that there will be a good outcome. The problem is that this unjustified belief is in stark conflict with what he knows about the case. Given his medical understanding of the symptoms it is patently irrational for him to expect a recovery. The tension between a realistic diagnosis and an optimistic expectation would produce a strange incoherence in the person's mind, almost a split personality. Would not a rational person find this conflict between evidence and belief intolerable? And if the belief stays firm must it not cast doubt on his understanding of the evidence? In that case he will probably look for alternative explanations of the symptoms, however farfetched, and focus on the slightest appearance of alleviation. Similarly, in Wittgenstein's example, it would appear to be a still more understandable response to find dubious reasons why past experience might after all yield some evidence for a better future (such as a Hegelian law of historical progress), than to believe in a better future flatly against all the evidence; that is, in effect, to expect a miracle.

Of course, the religious case is a little less problematic thanks to the transcendence of what is believed. There will be no conflict as to what one should expect to happen in this world (cf. IV. 4. & 6. above). Still, there is the same psychological problem. On Wittgenstein's account, the respectable theist is the one who is knowingly *not* reasonable in his religious beliefs (LC 58f.). But how can one believe what, at the same time, one believes is not likely to be true? – This is the unresolved tension in Wittgenstein's philosophy of religion. The tightrope walker's carefully limited abeyance of reason may not be objectionable; but is it possible? Hume famously claimed that 'whoever is moved by *Faith* to assent to [the *Christian Religion*], is conscious of a continued miracle in his own person, which subverts all the principles of his understanding' (131). With regard to the majority of religious people that is certainly not true; but it may be true of the consciously not reasonable believer Wittgenstein envisaged.[17]

Bibliography

R. B. Braithwaite, 'An Empiricist's View of the Nature of Religious Belief' in B. Mitchell (ed.), *The Philosophy of Religion*, Oxford: OUP, 1971; 72–91.

John Cottingham, *The Spiritual Dimension*, Cambridge, CUP, 2005.

—— 'What difference does it make? The nature and significance of theistic belief ', in *Ratio* XIX, 4; Dec 2006 (Special Issue: *The Meaning of Theism*, ed.: J. Cottingham); 401–20.

David Hume, *Enquires concerning Human Understanding and concerning the Principles of Morals*, Oxford: Clarendon Press, 1975.

John Hyman, 'The gospel according to Wittgenstein', in R. L. Arrington & M. Addis (eds), *Wittgenstein and Philosophy of Religion*, London: Routledge, 2001; 1–11.

William James, *The Varieties of Religious Experience*, London: Longmans, 1902.

J. L. Mackie, *The Miracle of Theism: Arguments for and against the existence of God*, Oxford: Clarendon Press, 1982.

D. Z. Phillips, *Wittgenstein and Religion*, Basingstoke: Macmillan, 1993.

Leo Tolstoy, *A Confession and Other Religious Writings*, Harmondsworth: Penguin, 1987.

Ludwig Wittgenstein:

B O. K. Bouwsma, *Wittgenstein: Conversations 1949–1951*, eds: J. L. Craft and R. E. Hustwit, Indianapolis: Hackett, 1986.

CV *Culture and Value*, rev. ed., ed.: G. H. von Wright, tr.: P. Winch, Oxford: Blackwell, 1998.

D *Denkbewegungen. Tagebücher 1930–1932/1936–1937 (MS 183)*, ed.: I. Somavilla, Innsbruck: Haymon, 1997. [Quoted by MS page numbers.]

E Paul Engelmann, *Letters from Ludwig Wittgenstein. With a Memoir*, tr.: B. F. McGuinness, Oxford: Blackwell, 1967.

---

[17] I am grateful to John Cottingham, David Dolby, and John Preston for critical comments.

GB 'Remarks on Frazer's *Golden Bough*', tr.: J. Beversluis, in *Philosophical Occasions 1912–1951*, eds: J. C. Klagge & A. Nordmann, Indianapolis: Hackett, 1993; 118–55.

LC *Lectures and Conversations on Aesthetics, Psychology and Religious Belief*, ed.: C. Barrett, Oxford: Blackwell, 1966.

LE 'A Lecture on Ethics', in *Philosophical Occasions 1912–1951*, eds: J. C. Klagge & A. Nordmann, Indianapolis: Hackett, 1993; 37–44.

M N. Malcolm, *Ludwig Wittgenstein: A Memoir*, 2nd. ed., Oxford: OUP, 1984.

OCD M. O'C. Drury, 'Some Notes on Conversations with Wittgenstein', 'Conversations with Wittgenstein', in R. Rhees (ed.), *Recollections of Wittgenstein*, Oxford: OUP, 1984; 76–171.

PI *Philosophical Investigations*, tr.: G. E. M. Anscombe, Oxford: Blackwell, 1958.

RR Rush Rhees, 'Postscript' in R. Rhees (ed.), *Recollections of Wittgenstein*, Oxford: OUP, 1984; 172–209.

TLP *Tractatus Logico-Philosophicus*, tr.: D. F. Pears & B. F. McGuinness, London: Routledge, 1961.

WVC *Wittgenstein and the Vienna Circle*, ed & tr.: B. F. McGuinness, Oxford: Blackwell, 1979.

6

RULES AND REASON

Joachim Schulte

Abstract

Wittgenstein's rule-following considerations (PI §§185–242) have often been discussed in terms of the debate occasioned by Kripke's interpretation of the so-called 'paradox' of rule-following. In the present paper, some of the remarks that stood in the centre of that debate are looked at from a very different perspective. First, it is suggested that these remarks are, among other things, meant to bring out that, to the extent we can speak of 'reason' in the context of rule-following, it is a very restricted form of reason – one which is basically to be understood as a kind of conformity. Second, by telling part of the story of the genesis of the relevant remarks it is pointed out that there is a certain tension between the 'liberating' character of earlier remarks bearing on rule-following (PI §§81ff.) and the 'sinister' side of later remarks like §§198–202, which helps explain why it took Wittgenstein such a long time to arrive at the views expressed in his rule-following considerations.

1. To speak of 'Wittgenstein's rule-following considerations' is to use a phrase which is fairly common in philosophical parlance. On most occasions of its use it is meant to refer to §§185 to 242 of the *Philosophical Investigations*. In many cases there is an implicit or explicit allusion to Saul Kripke's well-known treatment of these remarks, and those who intend such an allusion frequently make additional reference to writings by authors who in one way or another responded to Kripke, such as Warren Goldfarb, John McDowell, Colin McGinn and Crispin Wright. Other authors, and in particular those who tend to be sceptical of Kripke's approach and the responses of those who accept great parts of the framework established by Kripke's discussion, will turn to the writings of Gordon Baker, Peter Hacker and other scholars who, often by way of citing various passages from Wittgenstein's manuscripts, have expressed their feeling that Kripke was on the wrong track.

In this paper, I shall say nothing, or next to nothing, about these discussions and controversies. Like Kripke and many of the authors who responded to him, I think that §§185ff. of the *Inves-*

tigations are of great importance and interest; but I shall here emphasize reasons for regarding these remarks as important and interesting that are quite different from those adduced by Kripke. Like a few authors on various sides of this debate, I feel uncomfortable about the definiteness suggested by that phrase 'Wittgenstein's [or, perhaps, *the*] rule-following considerations'; even if we specify e.g. §§185 and 242 as clear limits of the sequence of remarks referred to, I am aware of too many different ways of subdividing this material and too many incompatible ways of reading individual remarks to be happy about the notion that we are dealing with a fairly well-defined argument. Like Baker and Hacker, I think that a close look at the manuscript sources won't hurt our understanding of Wittgenstein's train of thought; I diverge from their account by stressing different aspects of Wittgenstein's work.

To begin with, I want to mention two different starting points, each of which may help us arrive at the matters I should like to underline. The first point is the feeling that in the many years of discussing 'the rule-following considerations' or sifting Wittgenstein's *Nachlass* in the hope of finding the key to his remarks we have lost much of the ingenuousness required to notice some of the remarkable things suggested by these passages. We all remember the stubborn pupil who was first mentioned in §143 and later reintroduced in §185. So far he has made no mistake in reciting the number series '+2': he started by saying '0, 2, 4, 6 etc.' and did well up to '998, 1000'. Starting from here, however, he goes on by reciting '1004, 1008, 1012 etc.'. Of course, we try to correct him, but as we remember with chagrin, our efforts are not crowned with success. As a matter of fact, Wittgenstein points out that these efforts are based on ill-understood notions of meaning, knowledge and other central ideas. Now, what an unprejudiced reader may well be expected to say about this imaginary situation would be something along the following lines. 'The teacher has instructed the pupil in the use of certain rules. He has also corrected false moves on the part of the pupil and tried to point out to him where and in which way he went astray. Certain rules are standards of rationality; and if a person fails to live up to these standards, he thereby shows that he is not a rational kind of person. The rule "add 2" is surely a good candidate for a standard of rationality. So, if our pupil finds it impossible to apply it correctly, we should at a certain point decide to regard him as a consummate ass and treat him accordingly. In view of this, one wonders what all this fuss about meaning, agreement, the mind flowing ahead, steps taken in advance etc. could be about.' Now we have brought in reason (the second concept mentioned in my title), and I think this naive response is, even if its naivety is of the second-order kind, not to be discarded out of hand; it may actually be quite helpful to bear it in mind.

The second starting point is the history and (pre-history) of these remarks on rule-following. The manuscript of the first third of the *Investigations* was completed in the spring of the year 1937.[1] It was written in Wittgenstein's Norwegian cottage, and dictated to a typist in Vienna before his return to Norway in the autumn of the same year. In Norway Wittgenstein continued his work, but most of what he wrote in the following months was not what we know from reading the *Investigations*; most of this material is to be found in the *Remarks on the Foundations of Mathematics*, albeit in a thoroughly altered form. One of the most striking features of the early version of Wittgenstein's *Investigations* which resulted mostly from his Norwegian manuscripts written between November 1936 and December 1937 is the break in the middle of this version. The first half ends with the first paragraph of §189 and characteristically concludes with the words '*In der Frage liegt ein Fehler* – The question contains a mistake'. The second half begins with the very same paragraph and continues with a few remarks we know from the *Investigations*, but the bulk of that material is not to be found in the book. If you look at the typescript of the early version you can easily get the impression that the words 'The question contains a mistake' express Wittgenstein's feeling that he did not really know how to go on. The following remarks on what, mostly for reasons of convenience, may be called the philosophy of mathematics occasionally touch on the topic of rule following as broached in §§185ff., but they surely do not offer the sort of insights some of us find in the relevant part of the *Investigations*. As a matter of fact, it took Wittgenstein several years to arrive at these insights, and it may very well be that he needed to write all those remarks contained in his notebooks from the period between 1938 and 1943 or '44 before he could see the light reflected by §§189ff.

---

[1]   Cf. Joachim Schulte (ed., in collaboration with Heikki Nyman, Eike von Savigny, and Georg Henrik von Wright), Wittgenstein, *Philosophische Untersuchungen, Kritisch-genetische Edition*, Frankfurt am Main: Suhrkamp, 2001.

2. In a way Wittgenstein kept writing what he regarded as 'his book' since his return to Cambridge in 1929. His ideas were in constant flux, but if one is willing to put up with a certain degree of oversimplification, it may be quite helpful to divide up the development of his thought into short periods of a few years each. I think the most important break or turning point between 1929 and Wittgenstein's death in 1951 is the Norwegian period stretching from autumn 1936 to the end of 1937, which resulted in the early version of the *Investigations* comprising, roughly, the first 188 remarks of the book as we know it as well as most of the material in part I of the *Remarks on the Foundations of Mathematics*. The period before autumn 1936 is normally referred to as Wittgenstein's 'middle period', which in its turn can easily be subdivided into an earlier and a later part. The earlier part would cover the time up to the completion of what is generally called the 'Big Typescript' of 1933,[2] the later part could be seen to begin with the dictation of the *Blue Book* and to end with the German translation and revision of the *Brown Book*, which Wittgenstein worked on in the autumn of 1936 immediately before embarking on what became the first third of the *Investigations*. It is quite difficult to accommodate the various revisions of the 'Big Typescript' in terms of this scheme, but this need not bother us here.

Before proceeding to the time after 1937, let's have a look at the writings of the middle period to see if it is possible to characterise the ideas Wittgenstein had at that time about rules and rule-following. There is a huge number of remarks from that period either using the term 'rule' or discussing rules. What is striking when, with the *Investigations* in mind, one looks back at the writings from this period is that in the middle period there is a lot on rules but very little on rule-following. A typical question Wittgenstein considers at this time is 'What is the difference between a rule and a proposition?' (I follow the translators in using 'proposition' as the English equivalent of Wittgenstein's word '*Satz*', but I do so with grave misgivings.) He points out various respects in which an expression of a rule differs from an empirical statement while insisting that rules *describe* certain moves.[3] One way Wittgenstein devises to accom-

---

[2]   C. Grant Luckhart and Maximilian A. E. Aue (eds. and trans.), Wittgenstein, *The Big Typescript: TS 213*, Oxford: Blackwell, 2005.

[3]   Gordon Baker (ed.), Ludwig Wittgenstein and Friedrich Waismann, *The Voices of Wittgenstein: The Vienna Circle*, London and New York: Routledge, 2003, p. 262.

modate rules is by saying that rules are presuppositions of sense. A rule, he claims, is contained in the sense of a proposition, but rule and proposition do not form a logical product. This is the context where Wittgenstein develops his image of a proposition radical, well-known to readers of the *Investigations* (where the idea can be found in a note attached to §22). The following passage from Waismann's account of Wittgenstein's ideas sums this up:

> Rules belong to the preparation for propositions. Only in this sense can one say that the rule determines the sense of the proposition. The explanation of the words determines, e.g., the sense of the proposition. [. . .] If we say: rules are only means of representation, then we do not thereby want to maintain that propositions which describe certain uses or desires are means of representation. In this respect, ordinary language expresses itself clearly when it distinguishes the rule from the desire that the rule be complied with, hence, when it treats the rule as a propositional radical and not as a proposition.[4]

While the analogy between proposition radical and rule can be found in various places of Wittgenstein's manuscripts of that time, Waismann's notes contain a further image which I have not been able to trace in Wittgenstein's own writings. In Waismann's account, there are at least two passages where Wittgenstein compares the relation between rule and proposition with that between master and servant. He writes that

> if we want to distinguish a rule and a proposition, this is brought about by bringing the rule and the proposition together on the model of master and servant. If someone were to ask how master and servant differ, one could answer: if the master is dining, the servant is serving (but not: the master is dining, the servant is not). Master and servant are to be characterized by their *relationship*, and so too rule and proposition. If we give a statement of length, then we already presuppose a definition of the unit of length. Then one is inclined to say:

---

[4]   Ibid., p. 273.

This is really *only* a rule, by which one says, as it were: this is only the rule in the household of the proposition (where the proposition is the master).[5]

In his writings of this time Wittgenstein talks about all kinds of rules: rules of games, rules of a calculus and, above all, rules of language or grammar. In a number of places these rules of grammar are called 'conventions'.[6]

Another typical move is Wittgenstein's use of charts, tables, systems of arrows or sign-posts to exemplify the notion of a rule, and this is a move that can be found both in his middle-period writings and in later manuscripts. The tendency to use these illustrations is epitomized in §85 of the *Investigations*, where he says that 'a rule stands there like a sign-post'.

Often he compares the rules of games to the rules of grammar, and it is only on rare occasions that he wonders whether the comparison is really apt. In one passage from the 'Big Typescript' where he does wonder about this he admits that people who want to object to this analogy for the reason that e.g. the elements of competition, entertainment and recreation are absent in grammar are not mistaken. It may come as a surprise that Wittgenstein has not got much to say in reply to this objection. He insists that 'there obviously is some sort of similarity' between the rules of games and the rules of grammar. And he recommends that we look at both types of rules 'driven solely by the infallible instinct that there is a relationship here'.[7]

Clearly, this remark does not reveal much confidence in what is often regarded as a central idea of Wittgenstein's, viz. his comparison between the rules of games and grammatical rules – a comparison which is often believed to find its succinct expression in the idea of language-games. I emphasize this lack of confidence because I think that it foreshadows a slow transformation in Wittgenstein's attitude towards rules. In the early middle period he sees rules everywhere, and he is inclined to see everything in terms of rules, where his models tend to be fixed, specified or specifiable rules of the kind to be found in calculi and many games. Towards the end of this period and during the later middle period he talks

---

[5]   Ibid., pp. 271 / 273.
[6]   E.g. *Big Typescript*, §56.
[7]   *Big Typescript*, p. 238.

much less about rules,[8] but there is evidence that his ideas about rules are undergoing a change.

3. Part of this evidence is supplied by the history of a remark that can be seen as starting the first sustained discussion of the notion of a rule in the *Investigations*. It is at the same time a remark that introduces an idea which may be helpful in connecting rules and reason, viz. the idea of normativity. The remark I mean is §81 of the *Investigations*. It begins with the words 'F. P. Ramsey once emphasized in conversation with me that logic was a "normative science" '. Part of this remark originates in a manuscript entry of November 1931, which is repeated in the 'Big Typescript'. In both versions the opening words are similar to those we know from the *Investigations*, but the interesting bit about games, rules and comparisons is completely lacking. An early version of this missing bit was inserted in the process of a late revision of the 'Big Typescript', probably in the beginning of 1934, that is, at the time of dictating the *Blue Book*. Its wording was slightly changed when Wittgenstein worked this remark into the fabric of the early version of the *Investigations*. I shall now quote the relevant part of this paragraph in the form familiar to you, and then proceed to trying to explain what strikes me as noteworthy about it. Wittgenstein says:

> F. P. Ramsey once emphasized in conversation with me that logic was a 'normative science'. I do not know exactly what he had in mind, but it was doubtless closely related to what only dawned on me later: namely, that in philosophy we often *compare* the use of words with games and calculi which have fixed rules, but cannot say that someone who is using language *must* be playing such a game. –

Well, one thing that strikes me is the disingenuousness or glaring falsehood of these statements if they are taken literally. The first point is a minor one. We know, also from Wittgenstein's preface to the *Investigations*, that he had a large number of intense discussions with Ramsey about philosophical questions during the last year of Ramsey's life, that is, in 1929. So it is likely that he had a

---

[8]   See Wittgenstein, *The Blue and Brown Books*, Oxford: Blackwell, 1958.

fairly good idea of what Ramsey may have had in mind when he claimed that logic was a normative science. In particular, he must have known that Ramsey surely did not use the word 'logic' in the wide sense beloved by Wittgenstein, for whom it covered most of what he was doing in a philosophical way. He must also have known that, whatever Ramsey may have meant by his statement, it surely was *not* 'closely related' to the central idea expressed in the second half of my quotation. This second half commences with the glaring falsehood that in philosophy we *often* do what he then proceeds to describe as comparing the use of words with games and calculi that have fixed rules. Of course, in the 1930's there was very little philosophy, one might even say: virtually no philosophy, resembling Wittgenstein's description. Even if you take his own writings, only a very small part of them could be read as fitting this characterization. True, the *Brown Book* contains many sketches of games and what by courtesy might be called calculi; on the other hand, it does not bother much about *comparing* them to the uses of words.

That is not all that meets the eye when scrutinizing this quotation. But what are we to make of the part we have glanced at so far? I cannot really go into this question, but I shall give a brief, bipartite answer. The first part has to do with the fact (if it is a fact) that to some extent the *Investigations,* just like the *Tractatus,* is a very private book. Bringing in Ramsey is a way of calling him up from the dead, paying homage to his cleverness by expressing agreement, and teasing him by (nearly) attributing to him a view which was completely alien to him. The second part amounts to this: that the obvious falseness of at least some of what is said here indicates irony, and in Wittgenstein's writings irony often indicates that, in his view, at least some of the material presented is of great importance.

And I do think that the programmatic statement involved in this quotation is of the greatest importance. What it amounts to is, if I read it correctly, the following. When Wittgenstein says that 'in philosophy we often compare the use of words with games etc.' he means that *if* in philosophy we talk about games and calculi which have fixed rules, we should not understand this as applying directly to language and the use of linguistic expressions. We should understand it as an attempt at illuminating our use of words by way of bringing in more or less well-defined games and calculi that can serve as models or, as Wittgenstein likes to say, objects of comparison. These models or objects of comparison can come more or less near to what we really do with our words. But, as Wittgenstein continues to say in the same remark, it would be a serious mistake to regard our actual use of words as something that *merely* approximates those neater model language-games or objects of comparison – as if these were ideals to which our real linguistic exchanges could at best come close. The sense of 'model' needed here is that of an architect's scale model or an engineer's aeroplane model, not the sense of 'model which we are to copy or emulate'.

Another extremely important point is involved in the last part of the quoted passage, where Wittgenstein says that in philosophy we 'cannot say that someone who is using language *must* be playing such a game'. Now, the question of the real import of this statement is a very delicate one. On the one hand, it could mean that using language need not be an activity of exactly the same kind as operating a calculus or playing a game with explicitly defined rules that can be invoked at any stage of playing it. On the other hand, it could mean that using language need not be an activity that involves any kind of fixed rules. Of course, the second alternative can be read in all kinds of ways, but no doubt it is a stronger claim than that made by embracing the first alternative. If you lean, as I do, towards the second reading, you will have to accept a consequence you may not like. That is the consequence that the considerations put forward in §§185ff. do not, or need not, directly apply to our normal ways of using language, since *these* considerations do concern a calculus, a game with clearly fixed rules. To repeat: if you accept the stronger reading of the quoted passage from §81, the reflections of §§185ff. will turn out to be of indirect or remote relevance to questions of language use.

I can live with this consequence; in fact, I welcome it. But before I go on to another part of my discussion I want to point out two details of the passage quoted. Here, Wittgenstein says that the insight expressed in this remark 'only dawned on [him] later', that is, later than the time of his conversations with Ramsey. I take this as confirming a view I have argued for in various places[9]: the view that in the *Investigations* Wittgenstein distances himself not only, or not so much, from what he held at

[9]   Cf. for example my paper 'The Pneumatic Conception of Thought', in *Grazer Philosophische Studien*, 71 (2006), pp. 29–55.

the time of the *Tractatus* but also, or chiefly, from a number of
claims made and defended in the writings of his early middle
period.

The second detail is that the use of the word 'normative' suggested by Wittgenstein's remark is, to say the least, idiosyncratic. I
do not think that anyone else has ever used that word to declare
that fixed rules – standards or norms – need not play a role, and
that *comparisons* with rule-governed games or calculi are all that
is required by the 'normative' discipline of 'logic'. I think that
Wittgenstein means what he says here, and that what he says is to
be taken seriously. But we should remember that it is a very
unusual thing to say.

4. Let us go back to the history of the relevant portion of
the *Investigations*. I observed that the two typescripts forming the
pre-war version of the book display this striking feature: the end of
the first typescript is the first paragraph of §189 and thus concludes with the characteristic words 'The question contains a
mistake'. This paragraph is then repeated as the beginning of the
second typescript, which was, at a later stage, much revised and cut
into fragments that were then pieced together in a new order. The
result of this process is more or less what we know as part I of the
Remarks on the Foundations of Mathematics.

A few of the remarks contained in the second typescript
forming the pre-war version can also be found in the printed
Investigations, and it is not always clear in what way they were
meant to further the discussion of rule-following that was begun
in §185. One clearly gets the impression that Wittgenstein was
stuck. It is ironic that precisely at the point where he wonders
about the idea expressed by the words 'The steps are *really* already
taken' he does not know how to go on.

The discussion interrupted in §189 is continued in §198 and
culminates in §§199, 201 and 202. In these central remarks
Wittgenstein says that 'to obey a rule, to make a report, to give an
order, to play a game of chess, are *customs* (practices, institutions)'. The existence of such customs or practices is the
only connection between rule and action that Wittgenstein considers worth mentioning besides the purely causal one of training
people to go on in a certain way. He points out that rule-following
is not to be understood in terms of interpretation, that, on the
contrary, 'there is a way of grasping a rule which is not an interpretation, but which is exhibited in what we call "obeying the rule"

and "going against it" in actual cases'. These reflections are then summarized by the following statement:

> And hence also 'obeying a rule' is a practice. And to *think* one is obeying a rule is not to obey a rule. Hence it is not possible to obey a rule 'privately': otherwise thinking one was obeying a rule would be the same thing as obeying it.

Famous words, but why did it take Wittgenstein five years or so to arrive at them? I think the answer is not so difficult to find. These insights go very much against the grain. Wittgenstein cannot have found it easy to reach them as they lead to an attitude which in a certain sense appears to involve the abdication of reason.

Let me explain. And by way of explanation I should like to indicate a few points that can be found in the second (the as it were 'mathematical') part of the pre-war *Investigations*. Before getting down to these points I want to note that REASON is not the kind of notion Wittgenstein has much to say about. To be sure, there are remarks that can be construed as bearing on this notion; but there are very few that can be regarded as more or less explicit statements about this topic. However, there is an interesting observation that was written in the context of reflections on causality, at practically the same time Wittgenstein embarked on the manuscript notes that were eventually transformed into the first part of the *Remarks on the Foundations of Mathematics*, that is in October 1937. This observation can be seen as somehow connected with the Ramsey remark on normativity, which was quoted above, but it emphasizes a distractive aspect of the function of reason as a norm-setting power. Wittgenstein writes:

> Reason – I feel like saying – presents itself to us as the gauge *par excellence* against which everything that we do, all our language games, measure and judge themselves. – We may say: we are so exclusively preoccupied by contemplating a yardstick that we can't allow our gaze to *rest* on certain phenomena or patterns. We are used, as it were, to 'dismissing' these as irrational, as corresponding to a low state of intelligence, etc. The yardstick rivets our attention and keeps distracting us from these phenomena, as it were making us look beyond. – This is like the situation in which a certain style – a style of building or behaviour – captivates us to such an extent that we can't focus our

attention directly on another one, but can only glance at it obliquely.[10]

Reason as a faculty which sets standards and monitors their observance is here viewed as something that is far from exclusively beneficial. By attracting all our attention it prevents us from seeing alternatives and even stimulates us to dismiss unfamiliar practices as irrational. Thus it prevents us from exploiting the positive side of normativity mentioned in the above-quoted Ramsey remark: the opportunity of seeing our practices in the light of more or less analogous alternatives.

On the other hand, reason is what it is and can do what it does precisely in virtue of its limitations. Setting standards of rationality involves excluding alternatives as irrational, as not coming up to standards. In this sense, reason is a practice; its exercise is not as it were theoretical; it is simply going on the same way. *Interpretation* is a theoretical activity. It cannot rely on given standards but will have to respond in a flexible way to unprecedented situations.

This is what we did when we tried to deal with the stubborn student by trying to reason with him and attempting to point out to him that he was *not* going on as before. By doing this sort of thing we *may* be successful, as Wittgenstein says, but as long as we proceed in a theoretical fashion, i.e. by way of interpretation, we cannot be sure of being able to achieve anything: there is too little to refer to as a basis which could impress the stubborn pupil and *compel* him to go on the same way we do. In sum, 'any interpretation still hangs in the air along with what it interprets, and cannot give it any support'.

5. How did Wittgenstein arrive at this view? The path he followed took him past a number of variations on the theme of the stubborn pupil. But in particular he thought about various kinds of behaviour that would strike most of us as irrational or insane. Wittgenstein was fascinated by a passage from the preface to Frege's *Grundgesetze*, where the latter alludes to what he calls 'a hitherto unknown kind of madness'. On the other hand, Wittgenstein was disappointed by Frege's failure to spell out what he meant by this sort of madness. There is a challenge in this, and

---

[10] 'Cause and Effect: Intuitive Awareness', in *Philosophical Occasions*, ed. James Klagge and Alfred Nordmann, Indianapolis: Hackett, 1993, p. 389 (trans. modified).

Wittgenstein responds to this challenge by describing various scenarios of what, from our perspective, looks like irrational or mad behaviour. What is striking about these scenarios is that they do not describe an individual's deviant behaviour but unexpected practices of entire communities. Perhaps the best-known example is that of a people who sell wood, not by cubic measure or by weight, but by the size of the area it happens to cover. As Wittgenstein says, we *may* succeed in persuading these people to come round to our ways of selling wood. But as long as we do not use force but only words and arguments we have no compelling means of changing their behaviour.

A related example is that of a tribe whose members use what look like coins to pay for the goods they buy. But when it comes to paying they simply give the shopkeeper as many coins as they like while the shopkeeper gives his customers as much of the desired merchandise as they want. Again, this looks irrational to us but we know of no purely rational means of persuading them to behave otherwise. Many of us will feel inclined to say that, if the coins do not have the same function as in our culture, they will surely have some other purpose. But to this Wittgenstein responds by asking whether everything *we* do has a purpose. He reminds us of our own religious practices and of procedures like the coronation of a king. As he says, we are not prepared to 'call everyone insane who acts similarly within the forms of our culture, who uses words "without purpose" '.[11]

This sort of reflection persuades Wittgenstein that standards (including the standards of what we call 'rationality' or 'reason') tend to go together with our practices, entrenched forms of behaviour and customs of long standing. Conformity holds the key to the standards of reason; it may be that independent thinking is not futile, but ultimately it is powerless. Little wonder that it took Wittgenstein a long time to arrive at this view. There is no reason to suppose that he was entirely happy with it, but it chimed in with the acquiescent side of his thought.

6. Before I come to my, perhaps surprising, conclusion I should like to illustrate the difficulties Wittgenstein found in arriving at the view on rule-following expressed in §§198ff. of the *Investigations* by looking at a passage in the second half of the pre-war

---

[11] *Remarks on the Foundations of Mathematics* (= RFM), trans. G. E. M. Anscombe, Oxford: Blackwell, 2nd edition 1978, I §153.

version and its subsequent history. The passage I mean is a varia-
tion on the theme of the stubborn pupil. It is in dialogue form and
runs as follows:

> [A] 'But am I not compelled, then, to go the way I do in a chain
> of inferences?' – [B] Compelled? After all I can presumably go
> as I choose! – [A] 'But if you want to remain in accord with the
> rules you *must* go this way.' – [B] Not at all, I call *this* 'accord'.
> – [A] 'Then you have changed the meaning of the word
> 'accord', or the meaning of the rule.' – [B] No; – who says what
> 'change' and 'remaining the same' mean here?

> However many rules you give me – I give a rule which justifies
> *my* employment of your rules.

> [A] 'But you surely can't suddenly make a different application
> of the law now!' – [B] If my reply is: 'Oh yes of course, *that* is
> how I was applying it!' or: 'Oh! That's how I ought to have
> applied it –!'; then I am playing your game. But if I simply reply:
> 'Different? – But this surely *isn't* different!' – what will you do?[12]

This is the original little dialogue. One remarkable thing that
happened with it was that during the process of revision Wittgenstein inserted into this dialogue a sentence from a later page of his
typescript. This sentence runs: 'We might also say: when we follow
the laws of inference then following always involves interpretation
too.'[13] Of course, this conflicts with the tendency of what Wittgenstein says about rule-following and interpretation in the *Investigations*, and hence serves to show that around 1940 Wittgenstein still
had a long distance to travel before he could arrive at the position
embraced in the later work. Another interesting feature of the
process of revision of the quoted dialogue is the following. Probably around the same time he inserted the sentence about
interpretation he added a handwritten comment to the whole
dialogue. This comment runs: 'Basically this shows that a man who
displays signs of reason is also capable of acting in such a way that
we should call it foolish.' Two or three years later Wittgenstein
indicated that this comment was to be replaced by the following
note: 'That is: somebody may reply like a rational person and yet

---

[12] *Frühfassung* (TS 221) in *Kritisch-genetische Edition*, §§200–1. Trans. taken from RFM, I
§§113, 115. Evidently, the voice of B is used by Wittgenstein to make his point.
[13] RFM, I §114.

not be playing our game.'[14] It is one thing to say that people who appear rational may on occasion act in an irrational manner, and quite another thing to observe that a person who seems rational enough may refuse to play our game. By refusing to do so he may avoid all forms of intellectual defeat. On the other hand, he lays himself open to other forms of sanction if the members of his community do not wish to tolerate his deviant behaviour.

As I have said before, Wittgenstein does not have much to say about the philosophers' notion of REASON. In an unpublished paper, Lars Hertzberg expresses much the same view. He writes that while 'reason and rationality hold a place of honour in much of Western thought [. . .] Wittgenstein, on the other hand, never accorded these concepts so much as passing interest'.[15] In a footnote to this statement, Hertzberg points out that in Wittgenstein's last remarks, which were collected under the title *On Certainty*, the notion of a 'reasonable person' plays a certain role which, however, is quite different from that accorded it in standard philosophical writings.

This is entirely correct, and *On Certainty* is just where I wanted to arrive. On the one hand, quite a few of the images used in *On Certainty* recall the statement that 'any interpretation hangs in the air along with what it interprets'. In his last writings he not only speaks of foundation-walls which 'are carried by the whole house' (§248) and compares our world-picture to a mythology, which in its turn is compared to a river-bed in constant flux (§97); he also says that our most indubitable propositions are like an 'axis around which a body rotates' and which is 'not fixed in the sense that anything holds it fast, but the movement around it determines its immobility' (§152). One thing we may learn from these analogies is this: that an interpretation's hanging in the air is not such a terrible thing, after all; it shares its lot with a number of propositions which, according to the Wittgenstein of *On Certainty*, come nearest to playing the role of foundations, even though we must not forget that in the *Investigations* Wittgenstein insists that the interpretations mentioned there cannot give any support.[16]

---

[14] RFM, I §115.

[15] Lars Hertzberg, 'The Importance of Being Thoughtful' (unpublished typescript), p. 23.

[16] Cf. my paper 'Within a System', in Danièle Moyal-Sharrock and William H. Brenner (eds.), *Readings on Wittgenstein's On Certainty*, Houndmills: Palgrave Macmillan, 2005, pp. 59–75.

The second point is that the 'reasonable person' mentioned in various places in *On Certainty* is not a paragon of rationality but a stock figure, a character who used to be called 'the man in the street', exemplifying our normal attitudes towards what to count as certain or doubtful. It is in this sense that Wittgenstein says that 'we should not call anybody reasonable who believed something in despite of scientific evidence', and that 'When we say that we *know* that such and such . . . , we mean that any reasonable person in our position would also know it, that it would be a piece of unreason to doubt it' (§§324f.). In another passage he reminds us that 'what men consider reasonable or unreasonable alters. At certain periods men find reasonable what at other periods they found unreasonable. And vice versa' (§336). And he goes on to illustrate this by pointing out that '*very* intelligent and well-educated people believe in the story of creation in the Bible, while others hold it as proven false, and the grounds of the latter are well known to the former'. Again we are told that rationality, the standards of reasoning well, are bound up with certain practices in such a way that what is clearly reasonable to one man does not even impinge on what the other man believes or regards as self-evident.

In winding up I have to confess that I find this view troubling. I do not mean that I think it must be wrong. On the contrary, I am afraid that it is probably right, and it is this which I find troubling. Reason, which is embodied in our rules, e.g. in the rules of what we call scientific knowledge or morality, is in the same place where all the men in the street are. It can be impervious to what those who are not men in the street regard as reasons to think or act otherwise. And in this role it can serve to justify all kinds of sanctions that may be imposed against stubborn pupils.

I have always felt that there was something a little menacing about Wittgenstein's rule-following considerations. While I think that the tendency which comes to the fore in the Ramsey remark on normativity is highly liberating, the acquiescence informing the later material on rule-following may stifle our hopes that reason can do any work as an independent force. Fortunately, this is only a tiny part of the story about rule-following, but I thought it was worth mentioning.

7

RULE-FOLLOWING WITHOUT REASONS: WITTGENSTEIN'S QUIETISM AND THE CONSTITUTIVE QUESTION

Crispin Wright

Abstract
This is a short, and therefore necessarily very incomplete discussion of one of the great questions of modern philosophy. I return to a station at which an interpretative train of thought of mine came to a halt in a paper written almost 20 years ago, about Wittgenstein and Chomsky,[1] hoping to advance a little bit further down the track. The rule-following passages in the *Investigations* and *Remarks on the Foundations of Mathematics* in fact raise a number of distinct (though connected) issues about rules, meaning, objectivity, and reasons, whose conflation is encouraged by the standard caption, 'the Rule-following Considerations'.[2] Let me begin by explaining my focus here.

I. The rule-following dilemma

It is natural to think that in any area of human activity where there is a difference between *correct* and *incorrect* practice, which we achieve is (partly) determined by rules which fix what correct practice consists in, and which in some manner guide our aim. It also seems the merest platitude that wherever there are rules, there have to be *facts* about what their requirements are – and facts, moreover, which we are capable of knowing if the rules are ones whose guidance we are capable of receiving and acting on. Yet, as the rush of Wittgenstein-interpretative literature from the early 1980s onwards amply illustrates, the very idea of *facts about what rules require* seems on examination to raise a clutter of deeply perplexing questions of constitution and epistemic access. It is in the nature of rules, in a wide class of cases, to enjoin determinate mandates, permissions and prohibitions in

---

[1] Wright [1989]; reprinted in Wright [2001].
[2] – the caption was first introduced in my [1980], so I take some responsibility for such conflations as it may have encouraged.

previously unconsidered types of situation. So much seems to be no more than what is implicit in the idea that rules are things we *follow*: if we follow, then presumably they lead. But *how* do they manage to lead? In order for it to be possible for them to do so, it seems that three interrelated conditions have to be met. First (the *objectivity* condition), they have to issue their requirements independently and in advance of our appreciation of them; otherwise, there is no real leadership. But what kind of fact could it be that, in a context which no one has yet been placed in or considered, such-and-such a response, or course of action, is already what will be required by a particular rule? How in the world can such requirements be constituted? Second (the *relevance* condition), if a rule is to lead us, it has to be *that* rule rather than any other rule whose guidance we are accepting – there have to be facts about the identity of the specific rule we intend to follow. But how can that be? How and when can it have been settled that it is one specific rule in particular which we are following when everything we may so far have said, or explicitly thought, or done would be consistent with its being any of an indefinite number of potentially extensionally divergent rules?[3] And finally (the *epistemological* condition), even if rules are granted the proper independence seemingly demanded by the very idea of leadership, so that the facts about what is in accord with a rule or not really are fixed before any verdict of ours, and even if it is granted that we can once and for all somehow get one such specific, properly independent rule 'in mind', rather than any of an indefinite number of competitors, how can we account for our ability – in very many normal cases effortlessly, even thoughtlessly – to be appropriately sensitive to the specific requirements, case by case, of just that rule? *How* does a rule actually manage to lead us?[4]

These questions can seem both profound and misguided by turns. Certainly, there are tempting deflationary responses. For instance, it may be suggested concerning the objectivity condition that a rule – or at least, any rule of sufficient generality and

---

[3] This, of course, is the question prioritised by Kripke is his justly celebrated [1981].

[4] The overriding concerns about rule-following may thus be presented as an instance of what Christopher Peacocke in his [2000] termed the Integration Challenge: the challenge of '[reconciling] a plausible account of what is involved in the truth of statements of a given kind with a credible account of how we can know those statements, when we do know them.'

definiteness – is nothing if not something that precisely *does* mandate (or allow, or forbid) determinate courses of action in an indefinite range of cases that its practitioners will never have explicitly considered or prepared for. That is just what rules *are*. So there cannot be a legitimate puzzle about *how* a rule does that, or what settles what its requirements are. To ask how it is settled in advance what complies with the rule is like asking how it is settled what shape a particular geometrical figure has. The figure's shape is an *internal* property of it. What settles what shape the figure has is simply its being the figure it is.[5]

Yet the concerns merely reformulate and re-assert themselves. If a (suitably precise and general) rule is – by the very notion of 'rule', as it were – intrinsically such as to carry predeterminate verdicts for an open-ended range of occasions, and if grasping a rule is – by definition – an ability to keep track of those verdicts, step by step, then the prime question merely becomes: what makes it possible for there to *be* such things as rules, so conceived, at all? I can create a geometrical figure by drawing it. But how do I create something which carries pre-determinate instructions for an open range of situations that I do not think about in creating it? What gives it *this* rather than *that* content, when anything I say or do in explaining it will be open to an indefinite variety of conflicting interpretations? How can I make *it*, rather than a competitor, into an object which I intend to follow? And how is its content to be got 'into mind' and so made available to inform the successive responses of those who are to follow it?

Wittgenstein was conspicuously provoked by a certain way of thinking about these issues – perhaps better, a certain way of ignoring them – that he perceived as widespread in ordinary thought about logic and pure mathematics. The tendency in question could fairly be described as that of a kind of cavalier realism. It views logic and mathematics as tracking absolutely hard conceptual structures and interconnections. Discoveries in mathematics are regarded as the unpacking of (in the best case) deep but (always) predeterminate implications of the architecture of our understanding of basic mathematical concepts, as codified in intuitively apprehended axioms. And logical inference, for its part, is seen as the tracing of steps which are, in some sense, – in

---

[5]   John McDowell, for one, makes exactly this response in the context of the corresponding issue concerning intention – see pp. 163–4 of his [1991].

a favourite target image of his – *already* drawn and which we have no rational option but to acknowledge once presented to us. This way of thinking – it is, of course, Frege's way of thinking – conceives of the requirements of at least logical and mathematical rules as hyper-objective:[6] as somehow constituted quite independently of any propensities for judgement or reaction of ours. So an account seems needed of *how* they are constituted and of how we might reasonably presume ourselves capable of keeping intellectual track of their requirements so conceived.

It was, however – so I propose – a great achievement of Wittgenstein's to grasp the utter generality of this realist tendency and thus to notice that essentially the same way of thinking about the requirements of rules is quietly at work in much ordinary thinking about the mind; specifically, in the seemingly commonsensical yet notoriously troublesome idea that mental states and processes are items of direct acquaintance for their subjects but are strictly inaccessible to others, by whom they are knowable only by (potentially problematical) inference. It is a usually unremarked component in this to find no difficulty with the notion of simple *recognition* of the proper classification of one's own mental states and processes. Privacy is not supposed to be at odds with one's ability to conceptualise and articulate one's mental states for what they are – on the contrary, it is traditionally supposed to go hand in hand with the possibility of a special level of cognitive security in the judgements so articulated. Yet a judgement expressing a putative such recognition, insofar as it can be correct or incorrect, must presumably be a rule-governed response: there has to be a fact about what one *ought* to say of the targeted inner state – a fact about how it *ought* to be categorised, with which one's judgement about it is presumed capable, in the best (normal) case, of correspondence. So again it seems the question has to be faced: what constitutes such a fact? – what can make it the case that, independently of any reaction of mine, the rules of the language in which I give expression to my private mental life *mandate* certain types of description of an episode therein, and *prohibit* others; and what enables me to keep track of such requirements? Or again, if it is made constitutive of rules to carry such requirements and prohibitions: what can make it the case that specific such rules are associated with particular expressions in the

---

[6]   What Wittgenstein (*Philosophical Investigations* §192) styles 'superlative' facts.

language, and how can they be items of awareness for me in such a way that I can recognise what their specific requirements and prohibitions are?

In its most general form, the issue on which I want to focus here can be crystallised around my assent to any particular token statement, expressed in a language I understand, on a particular occasion of use. In order for this assent to be normatively constrained, and hence a candidate to be correct or incorrect, we have to be able to conceive of whatever constitutes its correctness or incorrectness as in some way independent of my disposition to assent. What are the candidates for such a 'requirement-constitutor'? The question confronts us with a broad dilemma. One thought – the *communitarian* response – is that the requirement-constitutor has somehow to be located *within* the propensities for assessment of the case possessed by others in my language community: that for my assent to the sentence in question to be – in the relevant context – in, or out, of line with the requirements imposed by its meaning is, in one way or another, for it to be in or out of line with others' impressions of those requirements. (Of course, this response cannot engage the case of descriptions of one's own mental states, viewed in the Cartesian way.) But the evident awkwardness with this idea is that it seems to reduce the correctness of an assessment to a kind of marching in step, and to exclude all room for the idea of judgements that are true anyway, no matter what we come to say about a question, or whether we even consider it at all. The other – *platonist* – response accordingly demurs: it says that even (hypothetically) shared assessments are constitutively quite independent of the requirements they concern – that even in the far-fetched scenario where a whole speech community assents to a particular utterance, and where everybody is clear-headed, attentive, and generally competent, the communal impression of what ought to be said is one thing and what really ought to be said is something else: something settled just between the character of the context and prevailing circumstances on the one hand and the meaning (the rules governing the use) of the statement in question on the other – and it should therefore be conceived as a matter on which a consensual verdict, even in the best epistemic circumstances, merely *alights*.

Our dilemma is, then, that prima facie there only seem to be these two options; but that the platonist – constitutional independence – line threatens to raise baffling ontological and epistemological problems; while communitarianism promises to struggle when it comes to recovering basic distinctions on which our ordinary ideas of objectivity, the growth of knowledge and the defeat of superstition seem to depend.

II Wittgenstein on the constitutive question

One response to the dilemma is to attempt to find a third way: to work out a conception of rules and rule-governed practices which allows sufficient of a gap between the requirements of a rule and subjects' reactions in any particular case to make sense of the idea of e.g. a whole community's misapplication of a rule they aim to follow, yet which stops short of any spurious, platonised idea of the autonomy of a rule and its requirements. That – specifically a proposal invoking a form of response-dependence – was the direction I took in the paper on Chomsky. But what does Wittgenstein himself think?

Well, it seems clear enough what he regards as the *sort* of considerations that should point us towards the right perspective on the problem. They are the considerations which constituted the last of four themes in the *Investigations* focused on in my [1989], which I there characterised in the following rubric:[7]

> *Language, and all rule-governed institutions, are founded not in our somehow internalising the same strongly autonomous, explanation-transcendent rules, whose requirements we then succeed, more or less, in collectively keeping track of, but in primitive dispositions of agreement in judgement and action.*[8]

One idea rejected here is that the idea of an essential inner process – a cognitive routine – common to all cases of rule-following is mythical. To express the matter dangerously, we need have nothing 'in mind' when we follow rules. The connection between the training in and explanations of rules which we receive and our subsequent practices is no doubt effected in ways which could only be sustained by conscious, thinking, intentional beings; but it is *not* mediated by the internalisation of explanation-

---

[7] Wright [1989] p. 243–4. I have tinkered with the wording somewhat.
[8] Illustrative passages include *Investigations* §§208–11, §§217–9, and §242; and *Remarks on the Foundations of Mathematics* VI, §39 and §49.

transcendent instructions that, in our training, we (something like) guessed at.[9] It is, for epistemological purposes, a *basic* fact about us that ordinary forms of explanation and training do succeed in perpetuating practices of various kinds – that there is a shared uptake, a disposition to concur in novel judgements involving the concepts in question. The mythology of 'rules as rails'[10] attempts an explanation of this fact. But the truth is the other way round: it is the basic disposition to agreement which sustains all rules and rule-governed institutions. The requirements which our rules impose upon us would not be violated if there were not this basic agreement; they would not so much as *exist.*

These aspects of Wittgenstein's thought are very familiar from the emphasis placed upon them in the secondary literature and, as the familiar often does, they can seem quite clear. But they are not clear. The difficulty is to stabilise the emphasis on basic propensities of judgement against a drift to a fatal simplification: the idea that the requirements of a rule, in any particular case, are simply *whatever we take them to be.* For if the requirements of the rule are not constituted, as the platonist thinks, independently of our reaction to the case, what can be available to constitute them *but* our reaction? But that idea effectively surrenders the notion of a requirement altogether. And Wittgenstein in any case explicitly cautions against it as a misreading of his intent.[11] So, what *is* his position?

---

[9]   *Investigations* §210.
[10] *Investigations* §218.
[11] Thus *Investigations* §241:

"So you are saying that human agreement decides what is true and what is false?" – It is what human beings *say* that is true and false; and they agree in the *language* they use. That is not agreement in opinions but in form of life.

Similarly *Remarks on the Foundations Of Mathematics* VII §40:

A language game: to bring something *else*; to bring the *same.* Now, we can imagine how it is played. – But how can I explain it to anyone? I can give him this training. – But then how does he know what he is to bring next time as 'the same' – with what justice can I say he has brought the right thing or the wrong? – Of course, I know very well that in certain cases people would turn on me with signs of opposition.

And does this mean e.g. that the definition of 'same' would be this: same is what all or most human beings with one voice take for the same? – Of course not.

For of course I don't make use of the agreement of human beings to affirm identity. What criterion do you use, then? None at all.

To use the word without a justification does not mean to use it wrongfully.

Again: Wittgenstein says that the requirements of rules exist only within a framework of ongoing institutional activities which depend upon basic human propensities to agree in judgement. But he also reminds himself that such requirements are also, in any particular case, understood as independent of our judgements, supplying standards in terms of which it may be right to regard those judgements, even when agreed, as incorrect. So we have been told what does *not* constitute the requirement of a rule in any particular case: it is *not* constituted by our agreement about the particular case, and it is *not* constituted autonomously, by a rule-as-rail, our ability to follow which would arguably[12] be epistemologically unaccountable. But we have not been told what *does* constitute it; all we have been told is that there would simply be no such requirements were it not for the phenomenon of actual, widespread human agreement in judgement. How can he possibly have thought that this was enough?

It is no good searching Wittgenstein's texts for a more concrete positive suggestion about the constitutive question. Indeed his entire later conception of philosophical method seems to be conditioned by a mistrust of such questions. Consensus cannot constitute the requirements of a rule because we leave space for – and do, on occasion, actually *make use* of – the notion of a consensus based on ignorance or a mistake. That is a distinction to which our ordinary practices allow content. The thing to guard against is the tendency to erect a mythological picture of the distinction's content, the myth about rule-following as the unaccountable tracking of 'superlative'[13] facts. The myth is active in the platonist philosophy of mathematics, and in the Cartesian philosophy of inner experience. So it is important to expose it. But, once exposed, Wittgenstein seems to be saying, it does not need to be *supplanted*:

> Our mistake is to look for an explanation where we ought to look at what happens as a 'proto-phenomenon'. That is, where we ought to have said: this language-game is played.[14]

No further *account* of the distinction – between an agreed move and a correct move – is necessary. Enough has been done when we

---

[12] Wright [1989] expounds what I take to be Wittgenstein's principal arguments to this effect.

[13] *Investigations* §192.

[14] *Investigations* §654.

have pointed out and defused philosophical misunderstandings of our linguistic practices in a way that avoids misdescription of their details. Our discourse of rules and meanings stands on its own feet. Platonism is a misunderstanding of it; but it does not need an alternative, better explanation to shore it up or otherwise account for the various locutions and distinctions which platonism misunderstands.

That, it seems, is his finished view.

III Whence the quietism?

The question I want to ask is: did Wittgenstein have any sound theoretical basis for this line? He is saying, in effect, that there is no well-conceived issue about the 'constitution' of facts about what rules require, instance by instance, or about what enables us to keep track of such facts. There is no real dilemma between platonist and communitarian views of the matter, and no constructive philosophical work to do by way of attempting to steer between its horns. But what is the ground for this claim – why should we agree with him?

The rubric above emphasised the *primitiveness* of our basic dispositions of classification and judgement. By this, I mean something coincident with – as I now propose to understand it – the metaphor of *blindness* that Wittgenstein introduces at *Investigations* §219.[15] Here is the passage in full:

> "All the steps are really already taken" means: I no longer have any choice. The rule, once stamped with a particular meaning, traces the lines along which it is to be followed through the whole of space. – But if something of this sort really were the case, how would it help?
> No; my description only made sense if it was to be understood symbolically. – I should have said: *This is how it strikes me.*
> When I obey a rule, I do not choose.
> I obey the rule *blindly.*

---

[15] In focusing on this metaphor, I follow a lead of Paul Boghossian (see the references to his work in the Bibliography) who has recently been laying emphasis on it in connection with the epistemology of basic logic, and foreshadowing a connection with the larger discussion of rule-following (see e.g. Boghossian [2003] at p. 237). He may or may not agree with the way I am going to develop it here.

What does Wittgenstein mean by saying that we follow rules *blindly*? Clearly, he is thinking of the simplest cases, where nothing takes place which can naturally be regarded as *working out* what a rule requires – cases where one's response seems to be immediate and one can produce no reason for it, no explicit justification. So the cases in point presumably include whatever rules are involved in, for example, the simple classification of colours, or tastes, or Lockean secondary qualities generally, as well as in some of the examples on which Wittgenstein tends to concentrate – judgements about the continuation of certain very simple diagrammatic or arithmetical series.

It would be a mistake, though, to take the point of the metaphor of 'blindness' as concerning the *phenomenology* of such judgements: in effect, as being that in making them (competently), *one is not aware* of any mediating process – of any route to the judgement which one might recover and cite by way of justification for it – but is just *smitten*, as it were, by the judgement. No doubt that is often so. But it cannot be the whole of the matter. In fact, I do not think it is the point at all. 'Blindness', after all, is a poor metaphor for *immediacy*, and the phenomenology in question is merely that of immediacy. The judgements of a sighted person about her local environment will include many immediate ones; they are hardly *blind* on that account. Wittgenstein's point is not (primarily) phenomenological. But then what is it?

Before we take that question head-on, we need to think further about the notion that sets our basic problem: the idea of the *facts* about what a given rule requires, allows or forbids in successive cases. Consider instead the more complex kind of case where one *does* reason one's way to a judgement about the proper application of a rule – for instance the case of Castling in chess. Here we find the following kind of structure of judgement.

> *Rule*: If neither King nor one of its Rooks has moved in the course of the game so far, and if the squares between them are unoccupied, and if neither the King nor any of those squares is in check to an opposing piece, then one may Castle
>
> *Premise*: In this game neither my King nor this Rook have yet been moved, the squares between them are unoccupied, and . . .
>
> *Conclusion*: I may castle now.

Call this the *modus ponens* model of rule-following.[16] The rule is stated in the form of a general conditional. A minor premise states that, in the circumstances in question, the condition articulated in the antecedent of the rule is met. The conclusion derives the mandate, prohibition, or permission concerned. Clearly, the model is of very wide application. In fact, I make so bold as to suggest that it applies, in essentials, in all cases when it is appropriate to think of one's impressions about what is in accordance with a rule as worked out, and when, correlatively, there *are* explicit reasons to be given for those impressions, by citing that working. Notice, however, that it is a feature of the model that one's knowledge of the rule is but *one* ingredient in one's movement to a correct application of the rule. There is a simple holism in operation, broadly akin to that involving belief and desire in the explanation of behaviour. Just as no behaviour, however bizarre, conclusively defeats the ascription to a subject of, say, a particular desire – you can always compensate by making sufficiently radical adjustments in the ascription of beliefs and other desires to her – so no response, however aberrant, in and of itself defeats the claim that a subject correctly understands and intends to follow a particular rule – you can always make compensatory adjustments by ascribing a misapprehension of the *initial conditions* for the application of a rule, as expressed in the minor premise in the modus ponens model. That makes it very easy to see that in cases where the model applies there can be no such thing as (what we may call) *pure* rule-following: that every judgement, or movement, made with the intent of compliance with a rule may go wrong not because the requirements of the rule are mistaken but – quite consistently with correct understanding of the rule – because of misapprehension of relevant features of the circumstances in which the rule is being applied.

Hard on the heels of that thought comes a generalisation: there is no pure rule-following not merely in cases that comfortably fit the modus ponens model but *anywhere*, however simple or basic the rule(s) involved. Even in cases, like the expansion of an arithmetical series, where there might be no *perceptual* input (because one is following the rule 'in one's head'), so no relevant risk of a perceptual mistake, judgements about the correctness, or permissibility of a next step will still depend on *memory*:

---

[16]   Cf. Wright [1989], p. 256

on not losing track of what one has so far done. To approximate a case of pure rule-following, one would need to consider a rule whose application involves neither perceptual input nor any memory of previous stages, nor even any extended process (of which one might lose track) in executing a single stage – so that each correct application at any stage can be made in a fully informed way without any sensory input or knowledge of any-thing else one has done or judged. There is no such case. The idea of pure rule-following – rule-following where a correct grasp of the rule is sufficient *tout court* to guarantee correct perfor-mance – is chimerical.

So what? Well, a key component of the problem of rule-following outlined in the first section above was the thought that if it is to be appropriate to think of an activity as subject to rule, then there have to be *facts* about what the relevant rules require, or permit, and – if we are to subject our practice to those rules – we have to be in position to know what these facts are. So ques-tions of the constitution and epistemology of such facts seem to be directly raised by the very idea of following a rule. We want to better understand how facts about the requirements of rules are made and how they are accessible to us. What the essential impu-rity of rule-following now raises is a question about what exactly *are* the 'facts about the requirements of rules' – what is their canoni-cal form of expression? If there is no pure rule-following, we cannot think of these facts as being the very same as the facts that make *particular* applications of rules, or judgements about what complies with them, correct. For the latter are always contami-nated by additional elements – concerning context, or history, or the input *to* which the rule is to be applied.

It may be replied that, at least in cases where the modus ponens model is apt, there are still isolable judgements about what prop-erly belongs to the rule and what belongs to the input provided by a situation in which an application of the rule is at issue. The separation is explicit in the model itself. What properly belongs to the rule corresponds to the conditional major premise in the modus ponens model – which will either be an explicit statement of the rule or a claimed consequence of one – while what corre-sponds to the situational input will be given by the minor premise. So the issues about constitution and epistemology may therefore intelligibly be focused on the former, or so it would seem. But the evident problem then, of course, is that this way of looking at the matter will not transpose to the basic – 'blind' – case. For in basic cases – the very simplest kinds of rule-following, gestured at above – the modus ponens model is inappropriate.

Wright [1989] reached a similar point –

> The ability successfully to follow a rule is thus to be viewed as, at each successive instance, the product of a number of cognitive responses which interact holistically in the production of the proper step. And some of these responses – correctly perceiving the set–up on the chess–board, for instance, or recollecting the expansion of the series to this point – do not strictly pertain to the rule but are possible for subjects who have no inkling of it –

but then observed something further:

> Where R is the rule or set of rules in question, let us call the [other responses]

– the ones that are *not* possible for subjects who have no inkling of the rule –

> *R–informed.* Now, an R–informed response need not be encap-sulable in any judgement which the subject can articulate dis-tinct from the output judgement, as it were – the judgement into which his or her R-informed and non-R-informed responses conjointly feed. In that respect, the chess example, in which the R- and non-R-informed components could be respectively explicitly entertained as the major and minor pre-mises for a *modus ponens* step, is untypical. I cannot always have concepts *other* than those whose governing rules I am trying to observe in a particular situation in terms of which I can formulate a separate judgement of the input to which these rules are to be applied. So I cannot always extricate and articulate a judgement which, conditionally on such a separ-ate judgement of the input, formulates my impression of the requirements of the rules in a fashion which is neutral with respect to the correctness of my R-uninformed responses to the situation.[17]

---

[17] Wright [1989] pp. 255–6.

So there is not just the *holism* to reckon with, blocking the possibility of pure rule-following. In addition, at least in basic cases, the contribution of grasp of the rule to the responses it informs is *inextricable* from the contribution of one's grasp of the prevailing circumstances. The clean separation effected by the modus ponens model between what belongs to the rule and what belongs to the situation to which it is to be applied is possible only in (relatively complex) cases where the conditions which trigger the application of the rule – those described in the antecedent of the relevant conditional – can be recognised and characterised in innocence of a mastery of the rule. That cannot be the situation in general.

My reaction to this consideration in the [1989] paper was to focus on the – for my purposes then – easier case where one's judgement about the requirements of a rule may be seen as resting upon extricable major and minor premises after the fashion of the modus ponens model.[18] Here, though – where our

---

[18]   The thesis I was there aiming to review was that, for the purposes of assessing any potential tension between the 'rule-following considerations' and 'the central project of theoretical linguistics', we should consider the impact of the former upon the status of the judgements – about grammaticality and content – which a systematic syntax and semantics for a natural language will generate concerning each of its strings. And a prime candidate for an encapsulation of that impact was, or so I argued, the thesis that such judgements were *response dependent*, that they failed 'the order of determination test': I wrote

> The test, as so far considered, calls for a class of judgements about which we can raise the question of the relation between best opinion and truth. And the existence of such judgements is just what the inextricability point counsels us not to expect in general. Still, there are extricable cases. The example of castling in chess provided one. And, most significant in the present context, the comprehending response to a novel utterance provides another. Such a response will involve a set of beliefs about the utterance which someone could have who had no understanding of the language in question; but it will also involve a belief about what, modulo the former set, has been said – a paradigm, it would seem, of a rule-informed judgement. Rather than confront the awkwardness presented by inextricability, therefore, let me concentrate for our present purposes on such favourable cases: cases where the acceptability of a rule-informed response can be seen as a matter of the truth of a judgement which the responder may be thought of as making. Our question, then, is: what makes for the truth of such rule-informed judgements?

– and the counselled answer was, roughly: their being made – or coinciding with the judgements that would be made – under conditions of *best* judgement. On this view, the well-formedness/meaning of a compound expression are not self-standing properties of it but are constituted in the very impressions of its well-formedness/meaning which competent speakers form under appropriate conditions. That was the suggested lesson of the rule-following considerations as applied to the Chomskyan/Davidsonian enterprise; and the consequent question was whether such a response-dependent conception of the con-

purpose is to try to get some kind of focus on the impact of Wittgenstein's rule-following discussion quite generally – we have no option but to attend instead to the harder range of cases, where the modus ponens model seems to lapse as a framework for the explanation of a rule-governed response, for the want of extricable major and minor premises.

Let us focus on the case of colour. Suppose, undeterred, we stubbornly try to assimilate predications of 'red' to the modus ponens model. The correctness of such a predication is thus to be seen as the progeny of an input condition of a certain character together with a rule associating such inputs precisely with the correctness of the predication:

Rule: If . . . x . . . , it is correct to predicate 'red' of x
Premise: . . . x . . .
Conclusion: It is correct to apply 'red' to x.

To conceive of predications of 'red' as rule-governed in the manner of the model accordingly requires an anterior concept, '. . . x . . .', whose satisfaction determines an input as appropriate for the application of the rule. But now it stares us in the face that this concept can hardly be anything other than: *red*! So we get an interesting upshot: the stubborn extension of the modus ponens model to the cases Wittgenstein would seem to have in mind when he speaks of rule-following as 'blind' would demand that we think of linguistic competence in terms, broadly, of the *Augustinian picture of language* with which the *Investigations* begins, and from which it is a journey of recoil. The crucial aspect of the Augustinian picture for our purposes here, of course, is not the confusion of meaning and naming which Wittgenstein himself fastens on in the immediately succeeding sections of the text, and on which his commentators have largely concentrated. It is the aspect, rather, that is highlighted a little later, at *Investigations* §32:

> . . . And now, I think, we can say: Augustine describes the learning of human language as if the child came into a strange country and did not understand the language of the country;

stitution of the syntactic and semantic properties of whole sentences left room for systematic syntax and semantics as genuinely explanatory empirical theories in the manner their principal architects had conceived.

That, by the way, still seems to me to be a fascinating, under-discussed question. For one recent, helpful discussion of it, see Miller [forthcoming].

that is, as if it already had a language, only not this one. Or
again: as if the child could already *think*, only not yet speak. And
'think' would here mean something like 'talk to itself'.

In short, the problem with extending the modus ponens model to
cover all rule-following, including that involved in basic cases, is
that it calls for a conceptual repertoire *anterior* to an understanding of any particular rule – the conceptual repertoire needed to
grasp the input conditions, and the association of them which the
rule effects with a certain mandated, prohibited or permissible
form of response. From the standpoint of the philosophy of
thought and language of the *Investigations*, this is an enormous
mistake. With respect to a wide class of concepts, a grasp of them
is not anterior to the ability to give them competent linguistic
expression but rather *resides in* that very ability. (This need not be
a commitment to holding that there is never any sense at all to be
made of the idea of thought without language. But it is to repu-
diate the *general* picture of thought as an activity of the mind
which language merely clothes.)

If this is right, then a crucial component of Wittgenstein's
thought about rule-following depends upon a perspective which,
more than half a century after he put his ideas to paper, seems to
have come – one may well feel: regrettably – to appear non-
compulsory to many contemporary philosophers of mind: the
conception of language not merely as a *medium for the expression* of
thought but as – usually, though not exceptionlessly – *enabling*
thought: as providing its very raw materials. From this perspective,
the modus ponens model *must* lapse for basic cases. Basic cases –
where rule-following is 'blind' – are cases where rule-following is
uninformed by anterior reason-giving judgement – just like the attempts
of a blind man to navigate in a strange environment.[19] In such a case
one follows a rule 'without reasons' in the precise sense that one's
judgements about the input condition for correct application of
the rule are not informed by the exercise of concepts other than
that which the rule concerns – that is, the concept whose expression the rule regulates and grasp of which consists in competence
with that very expression. Such a judgement is an ungrounded

---

[19] Of course, the analogy limps immediately after this point – the movements of the
blind man will naturally be hesitant. But in basic rule-following 'I act quickly, with perfect
certainty, and the lack of reasons does not trouble me' (*Investigations* §212.)

response in the precise sense that is not to be rationalised by the modus ponens (as I have suggested: the only possible) model – by the picture of rule and input as (potential) components of independent thought. It is still essentially the response of a rational subject, and still to be appraised within the *categories* of rationality – justification and truth. But it is an action for which, it is now tempting to say, the subject has and can have no reason – for the possession of such reasons and their appreciation as such would demand the exercise of an anterior concept, in an independent judgement, of what made the action appropriate.[20]

So here is what seems to be the resulting position. All rule-following involves basic rule-following. And basic – 'blind' – rule-following, properly understood, is rule-following without reason – not in the sense of being phenomenologically immediate, or spontaneous in the way in which a good chess player may make a clever move without fully self-consciously rationalising his grounds for it, but in a sense involving the inappropriateness of the modus ponens model. But that model represents the only extant shot – once again, I'm tempted to say, 'the only possible shot' – at the extrication of a class of judgements which would distinctively express the special facts about what rules require that the very idea of normativity seems to call for, and which – if we could somehow extricate them – would provide the necessary focal point for the issues concerning constitution and epistemology at the core of the problematic about rule-following with which we started. So there *has to be something wrong* with that problematic. And what is wrong, one might say, is that in the basic case we do not really *follow* – are not really guided by – anything. The problematic invited us to try to construct an account of what, when we follow a particular rule, constitutes the facts about the direction in which, step by step, it guides us and how we are able to be responsive to its guidance. But in basic cases the invitation emerges, from the perspective on the matter just adumbrated, as utterly misconceived; for it presupposes a false conception of the sense in which basic rule-following is rational. Basic rule-following, like all rule following, is rational in

---

[20] A similar point should apply, if good, to the exercise of the concepts in the background repertoire with which Augustine accredits us. In basic cases, such exercises too will be blind: for it cannot always be that one's application of a concept is grounded in thoughts that involve the use of other concepts. What is not clear is whether thought, so conceived, should be regarded as involving the following of rules at all. (But that's a can of worms which I won't open here.)

the sense that it involves intentionality and a willingness to accept correction in the light of error. But that is not to say that it involves responsiveness to the requirements of the rule, conceived as instructions, as it were, which can feature in thought and rationally inform one's response. The initial problematic – what constitutes the requirements of rules and how are we able to keep track of them – presupposes otherwise.

In summary: To say that in basic cases, we follow rules blindly or without reasons is to say that our moves are uninformed by – are not the rational output of – any appreciation of *facts about what the rules require*. This is, emphatically, not the claim that it is inappropriate ever to describe someone as, say, knowing the rule(s) for the use of 'red', or as knowing what such a rule requires. Rather, it is a caution about how to understand such descriptions – or better: about how *not* to understand them. In any basic case, the lapse of the modus ponens model means that we should not think of knowledge of the requirements of the rule as a state which *rationally underlies* and enables competence, as knowledge of the rule for castling rationally underlies a chess player's successfully restricting the cases where she attempts to castle to situations where it is legal to do so. In basic cases there is no such underlying, rationalising knowledge enabling the competence. *A fortiori* there is no metaphysical issue about the character of the facts it is knowledge of, with platonism and communitarianism presenting the horns of a dilemma. The knowledge *is* the competence. Or so I take Wittgenstein to be saying.

That is why Wittgenstein's own response to his well-argued rejection of platonism is quietist. A non-quietist response would be called for only if platonism had given a bad answer to a good question. Then one would have to try to give a better answer. But the question was bad too. The real error in platonism is not the unsustainability of its sublimated conception of rule-facts, or the vulnerable epistemology that attends the sublimation. Rather the whole conception of rule-following to which it was a response was already an over-rationalisation – an implicit attempt to impose on rule-following everywhere a rational structure which can only engage the non-basic case.

IV Rational judgements made for no reasons?

There is no doubt that the general tendency of the foregoing discussion goes deeply against the grain. Normal thought envelops even our basic judgements with a *rhetoric* of reasons. I assent to the judgement that something is red. You ask me: what reason do you have to think so? I can perfectly properly answer, 'Well, the way it looks, of course'. But *how* does the look serve as a reason? In response, one immediately finds oneself thinking in terms of the modus ponens model: 'Well, the object has a certain look; it is constitutive of the concept *red* that things that look that way are (defeasibly) appropriately taken to be red. Therefore, the object in question may appropriately be taken to be red.' But this is just the model that in basic cases we have discarded.

There are considerations that one may marshal to try to sugar the pill. Suppose I assent to a judgement about something's colour, based purely on its look. In what sense is this assent rational? One can say several things:

That it is an act possible only for a creature that is rational;
That it is an act in the 'space of' reasons – open to assessment as correct, responsibly made, and so on;
That it is an act that may in turn contribute to my reasons for (other) acts and judgements.

But these considerations are all broadly concerned with the stage-setting and implications of the act: with how I must be regarded if I am credited with that very act, with how it may be appraised, and with what it commits me to. They do nothing, it seems, to restore the idea of the *input-rationality* of basic judgement – to explain how a basic judgement can be made on the basis of reasons which the thinker *has*, how it can be the *product* of a rational response to anterior, reason-giving states.

It is clear where pressure would have to be exerted if the lost ground is to be (even partially) regained. Means would have to be provided to distinguish the conclusion that basic judgements are judgements made for *no reason that can be captured via the modus ponens model* from the stronger conclusion that they are made for *no reason at all*. I have been suggesting that the modus ponens model supplies the only means whereby facts about the requirements of rules can enter into a subject's reasons for an act, – that it is only in terms of the model that we can make sense of the idea of the rationality of a judgement or action if it is to be conceived as the product of following a rule. If that is right, and if basic judgements are nevertheless input-rational, then the conclusion is clear: we have to understand them as rationalised in a way that takes them *outside* the category of rule-following. If basic judge-ments are judgements made for no reasons involving rational processing of information about the requirements of rules, and if they are nevertheless made for reasons, they are not to be thought of as delivered by the following of rules. (And of course, if they are made for no reasons, then they are not to be thought of as delivered by the following of rules in any case.)

So how might we try to regard them instead? What kind of nature and structure might their reasons have if not that of the modus ponens model? There is one well-documented but, as it has proved, vexed proposal. As remarked, it is our normal rhetoric to say that it is looks – more generally, *experiences* – that rationalise our most basic empirical judgements. However, if experiences are to do this, then they have to possess attributes which fit them to do so. What kind of attributes would accomplish that? The modus ponens model will have it that, whatever they are, they will need connection, via a major premise presumed to be already part of the thinker's information, with the appropriateness of the judge-ment the experience rationalises. If this is to be avoided, there must be no role for such a major premise. Therefore, experiences must have attributes which fit them to rationalise empirical judge-ments *immediately* – that is, without any kind of rational interme-diary processing of thoughts. The idea is then apt to seem compelling that such rationalisation can be accomplished only if we conceive of experience as already *essentially conceptually content-ful*: experience has essentially to consist in the reception of appearances that . . . , where what fills in the dots is a conceptual content. There has to be such a content because otherwise it is obscure how experience can *rationalise* judgement, rather than merely causally predispose to it; and the content has to be carried essentially since otherwise the assignment of content to an expe-rience would have to proceed by principles connecting 'given', non-contentual characteristics with content – and that would take us straight back to the modus ponens model.

Such is, of course, exactly the conception of experience pro-pounded in John McDowell's *Mind and World*.[21] McDowell's route into it is, familiarly, different: he presents it as a *via media* to avoid the unsatisfactory answers to the question, how can empirical judgements be rational, offered respectively by the (putative)

[21]   McDowell [1994]

Myth of the (non-conceptual, sensory) Given and Davidsonian coherentism. However, if what I have said is right, McDowell's conception of experience is actually mandatory for any philosopher determined to have it that basic judgements are made for reasons furnished by experience.

It is another question, of course, whether the conception is stable or satisfactory.[22] Common complaints have concerned its apparent exclusion of the experience of infants and animals and the lack of any foreseeable principled account of which are the contents that experience can carry intrinsically (not presumably, for example, that this object is a geiger-counter . . .) However, a more urgent question about it now, in the light of the preceding discussion, is *how* experiences come to be fitted out with the conceptual contents which, according to the McDowellian idea, they essentially carry. Labeling the conceptual content of experiences 'essential' to them is, for the reasons just gestured at, a forced move. But it is a major concern whether there is any way of making sense of the idea which is not at odds with the broader lessons of Wittgenstein's discussion. For if experience is to be intrinsically such as to rationalise judgement, it must carry the content it does *independently* of judgement. And how is that idea to be sustained except at the cost of crediting the concepts configured in an experience's content with a kind of platonic propensity to self-application?

The issues waiting in this direction must be material for another discussion.[23]

Bibliography

P. Boghossian, 'Knowledge of Logic', in P. Boghossian and C. Peacocke (eds.) *New Essays on the A Priori* (Oxford: Oxford University Press, 2000) pp. 229–254.

—— 'How are Objective Epistemic Reasons Possible?' in J. Bermúdez and A. Millar (eds.), *Reason and Nature: Essays in the Theory of Rationality* (Oxford: Clarendon Press, 2002) pp. 15–48.

[22] My own previous contributions to the extensive commentary include Wright [1996] and [2002].

[23] Precursors of this material have been presented at various seminars and colloquia including the European Summer School in Analytical Philosophy held at Parma in 2001, the Mind and Language seminar at NYU in spring 2002, the May meeting of the Scots Philosophical Club, and the Reading one-day conference on *Wittgenstein and Reason* in 2006. Thanks to the discussants on all these occasions. Special thanks to Paul Boghossian, Cyrus Panjvani and John Skorupski for detailed discussion and comments.

—— 'Blind Reasoning', *Supplement to the Proceedings of the Aristotelian Society* 77, 2003, pp. 225–48.

—— 'Blind Rule Following', in A. Coliva (ed.), *Mind, Meaning and Knowledge: Essays for Crispin Wright Volume I* (Oxford: Oxford University Press, forthcoming).

S. Kripke, *Wittgenstein on Rules and Private Language* (Oxford: Basil Blackwell, 1981).

J. McDowell, 'Intentionality and Interiority in Wittgenstein' in K. Puhl (ed.), *Meaning Scepticism* (Berlin: de Gruyter, 1991), pp. 148–69.

—— *Mind and World* (Oxford: Oxford University Press, 1994).

A. Miller, 'Critical Notice of Wright (2001)', *International Journal of Philosophical Studies* (forthcoming).

C. Peacocke, *Being Known* (Oxford: Oxford University Press, 2000).

C. Wright, *Wittgenstein on the Foundations of Mathematics* (London: Duckworth, 1980).

—— 'Wittgenstein's Rule-following Considerations and the Central Project of Theoretical Linguistics', in A. George (ed.), *Reflections on Chomsky* (Oxford and New York: Basil Blackwell, 1989), pp. 233–64.

—— 'Human Nature?' (critical study of John McDowell's *Mind and World*), *European Journal of Philosophy* 4, 1996, pp. 235–54.

—— *Rails to Infinity*, (Cambridge, Mass., Harvard University Press, 2001).

—— Reprint of 'Human Nature' with a new postscript in N. Smith (ed.), *Reading McDowell: On Mind and World* (London: Routledge, 2002) pp. 140–73.

L. Wittgenstein, *Philosophical Investigations*, 3rd edition (Oxford: Basil Blackwell 1967).

—— *Remarks on the Foundations of Mathematics*, 3rd edition (Oxford: Basil Blackwell 1981).

INDEX

Note: Wittgenstein's works are shown in **bold**.

Printed and bound by CPI Group (UK) Ltd, Croydon, CR0 4YY

13/04/2025

14656462-0004